20-40-60
minute dinners

MEALS TO MATCH THE TIME YOU HAVE

Kate Otterstrom the creator of the Dinner in Real Time blog

SHADOW MOUNTAIN PUBLISHING

For Mom and Dad,
in gratitude for a lifetime of
unflagging support and love.

Food photography by Kate Otterstrom. Illustrations by Inge Otterstrom.

Any trademarks, service marks, product names, or named features are the property of their respective owners, and they are used herein for reference and comparison purposes only. This book was not prepared, approved, licensed, or endorsed by any of the owners of the trademarks or brand names referred to in this book. There is no express or implied endorsement for any products or services mentioned in this publication.

Visit us at shadowmountain.com

Library of Congress Cataloging-in-Publication Data

Names: Otterstrom, Kate, author.
Title: 20–40–60-minute dinners: meals to match the time you have / Kate Otterstrom, the creator of The Provident Table blog.
Description: [Salt Lake City]: Shadow Mountain Publishing, [2023] | Includes index. | Summary: "Whether you only have twenty minutes or an hour—or something in between—you can deliver a delicious entrée and side dish to the table with these quick, easy, and crowd-pleasing recipes. Organized by "available time" rather than by "kind of dish," this unique cookbook is designed to help the time-conscious cook with dinner planning. Since Kate is gluten-intolerant herself, each recipe also includes instructions on how to adapt it for a gluten-free option."—Provided by publisher.
Identifiers: LCCN 2022043084 | ISBN 9781639931095 (trade paperback)
Subjects: LCSH: Quick and easy cooking. | Gluten-free diet—Recipes. | BISAC: COOKING / Methods / Quick & Easy | COOKING / Comfort Food | LCGFT: Cookbooks.
Classification: LCC TX833.5. O875 2023 | DDC 641.5/12—dc23/eng/20221021
LC record available at https://lccn.loc.gov/2022043084

Printed in China
RR Donnelley, Dongguan, China

10 9 8 7 6 5 4 3 2 1

Contents

It's Time for Dinner!

I have always enjoyed cooking and baking, and I find satisfaction in making things that other people like to eat. Like many kids, I enjoyed making cookies and decorating gingerbread houses. As a high-school student I pushed my boundaries by experimenting with flavors and ingredients. In college I cooked in a kind of distracted, impulsive way that was often just for survival, but occasionally I aimed to produce a special treat. Throughout all of this, I never did much planning until I got married and started cooking on a daily basis for my small family. I quickly realized the power of a good menu plan as part of both keeping the budget and keeping the peace! As life has become more complicated with the arrival of each of my four children, increased community and church responsibilities, and my husband's demanding career, menu plans have become essential.

Learning to plan menus has not been easy. I have struggled with too much information, dietary restrictions, recipes that sounded interesting but didn't seem to fit my budget or time constraints, recipes that sounded interesting but turned out to be duds, concerns about conservation of natural resources and the impact of what my family was eating on our planet, and how to figure out the timing of it all. It gets difficult to plan a single cohesive dinner with so many issues competing for your attention. Perhaps I overthink it all, but I can't get beyond the reality that what I eat is a reflection of who I am and what I care about. That, and I want to make sure my kids are eating their vegetables.

As I talk about food and cooking with friends, I've found that almost everyone struggles with some form of these concerns. Schedules vary, resources and diets make things complicated, and, as a result, good intentions to gather for a homemade dinner too often devolve into stressful moments and a trip to the favorite fast-food joint. With a little tailored planning, dinner does not have to be this way. It can be a time for nourishment and conversation without undue stress—consistently and dependably providing space for the moments of connection that we all need.

20–40–60-Minute Dinners is organized by timing, rather than by the conventional appetizer, soups, salads, meats, and so forth organization. Within each timing category I've included some of my favorite recipes. This will allow you to easily reference dinners that will work with your schedule, without getting lost among other attractive recipes that will just not fit at the time.

I have written my recipes as complete menus in tables, intending to keep the recipes interruption-proof and allow you to streamline your time. You can proceed through the recipe efficiently and use the time while one component is cooking to prepare other components in a time-optimizing order. By using a table format with ingredients listed in the left-hand column and directions for those ingredients in the right-hand column, you can cook in the real world of a kitchen where interruptions are likely and *mise en place* is a pipe dream. This format makes it easy to figure out where you are, and where that ½ teaspoon of salt goes, should you be interrupted by a yowling cat who thinks that the world will end if he doesn't get put out/fed/petted immediately, or by kids arguing and coming dangerously close to physical contact, or by the dog barking at the flowerpot on your neighbor's porch—or any of the other interruptions that arise every time you try to focus on just making dinner.

These recipes are written to make enough food to feed 4–8 people, depending on the recipe (there are specific notes about servings in the recipe headnotes). They are also easily halved if you need to prepare dinner for fewer than the number of people indicated in the recipe.

Finally, I have adapted my recipes to be gluten-free if desired. I was diagnosed with celiac disease as an adult. My diagnosis has required me to find new ways to cook and bake, and I've included modified instructions here for every recipe. One crucial note: If you are cooking or baking for someone with a food allergy, please be sure to wash everything, including mixing equipment, with soap and water. Cross-contamination is a real problem when it comes to celiac disease and other food allergies.

I hope that this time-centered approach will help you find greater satisfaction and success in making and taking your daily bread. I echo Julia Child's exclamation in wishing you *bon appétit*, but just as importantly I hope you experience *bon préparation*!

Your Recipe File

Most of the time I find myself restricted in my recipe selection by my schedule rather than by ingredients. I've organized this cookbook in sections that reflect time constraints. The first time-constraint category, *College-Style Dinners*, contains recipes that can be prepared between 20 and 35 minutes of collecting ingredients from your well-stocked pantry or a quick trip to the closest grocery store. The next time-constraint category is *Quick-Prep Dinners*, which includes meals you can make from basic ingredients in about an hour.

Then we get into sections that aren't quite so time-constrained. The first of these is *Slow-Cooker Dinners: For When You're Coming In Hot or Exhausted*, which is organized by prep time, since the actual cooking takes place as you're out doing other things. The next is *Frozen Dinners: When You Give Yourself a Present*, also organized by prep time; these recipes are written so that you can either make them ahead of time and freeze them—or double them, eat one and freeze the second, then pull the extra out on a night when you only have time to reheat something. The next is *Time-Consuming Dinners: Labors of Love and Flights of Fancy*, organized by total time—but these recipes are lavish meals for special occasions when you have from two hours to a whole day to prepare. *Accompaniments: Mostly Vegetables* are side dishes and salads for when you find you have a little extra time. *Breakfast: Here We Go Again!* is self-explanatory. The final section, *Baking and Candy: Comfort and Magic*, includes essential baking and candy recipes that vary in time between 30 minutes to 8 hours.

You can personalize your book by making notes in the margins to better visualize how your favorite recipes fit into these time categories. As you use these recipes and notes in your menu planning, you will be able to choose recipes that will fit neatly into your day and not be a source of stress. It's time to reclaim dinnertime!

Your Kitchen

It can be helpful when you pick up a new cookbook to know what equipment will be required to cook and bake the recipes included in the cookbook. I prefer to keep a relatively spare kitchen. Here is a list of essential equipment, as well as a few extra items that I believe are worthy of taking up space in my kitchen.

Kitchen range: I cook on and in an electric glass-top range with a large single oven. While the cooktop is not as responsive as gas, it is very easy to clean, and the oven is much more predictable than a gas model.

Baking stone and wooden peel: Because the baking stone makes such a difference in getting a crisp crust on gluten-free breads and pizzas, I keep mine in my oven all of the time. The peel is essential for getting things on and off of the stone without burning yourself.

Microwave oven: While this is not strictly essential, it can save a great deal of time and energy when it comes to defrosting, melting, or softening cold ingredients.

Toaster oven: When a small quantity of bread needs to be toasted in a recipe, it's nice to be able to use the toaster oven rather than heating up the whole oven.

Electric griddle: While not entirely essential if you have a nonstick sauté pan, an electric griddle is a huge time-saver when making pancakes and flatbreads.

Thermometers: I have both an *instant-read thermometer* and a *candy thermometer*. Both are essential.

Rice cooker: When my husband asked my Japanese friend which rice cooker was her favorite and then purchased it for my birthday, I felt lucky indeed. Rice cookers are definitely not essential, but they make your life much easier and can produce superior rice. Pressure cookers or multicookers can do the job, but I prefer my Zojirushi!

Stainless steel steamer basket: This small folding basket fits inside a saucepan and allows for steaming vegetables, eggs, and even rice without the food coming in contact with the water.

Slow cooker: This is an essential tool for making dinner that will be ready for you when you come home after a long day. Most multicookers also have a slow cooker function.

Refrigerator: Every once in a while when I hear horror stories of refrigerators failing and food going bad, I am reminded of what a luxury it is to have a refrigerator to avoid having to shop or consume any leftovers every day.

Food scale: Weighing flour is much more accurate than using volumetric cups because of the way flour tends to pack. You have likely heard bakers recommend the food scale and seen them used on baking shows. Food scales really are the best way to measure baking ingredients and ensure success with the recipe.

Measuring spoons and liquid measuring cups: For measuring things like salt and leavening agents, measuring spoons are still my preferred choice. Liquid measuring cups designed to see quantities from the top rather than the side are helpful.

Mixing bowls—large, medium and small: I have three mixing bowls and use them all for different recipes. Having a range of bowls is helpful if you have the space.

Stand mixer: This received essential status when I began working with gluten-free doughs, which tend to be too sticky to knead but too stiff to stir by hand for very long.

Whisks: I have a few different shapes and sizes of whisks for necessary mixing. I love whisks!

Rolling pin: Find a nice heavy rolling pin. I prefer wood.

Colander: Essential for draining pasta and beans.

Fine mesh sieve: This can be a good option for draining excess liquid and can double up for scattering fine dry ingredients such as powdered sugar or cocoa.

8-inch chef's knife, 3½-inch paring knife, serrated knife: I purchased good knives several years ago and have never regretted them. Also essential to safe knife use is an **electric knife sharpener** and lessons about holding knives properly, which you can find online by searching for "proper knife technique."

Cutting boards: It is helpful to have more than one if you have the space.

Kitchen shears: These are necessary to have around for cutting up poultry and cutting open packages.

Pizza wheel: This little tool is surprisingly versatile when cutting up doughs.

Grater and zester: For cheese and citrus, a good grater and zester is essential. I prefer a hand grater that has a variety of grating surfaces.

Vegetable peeler: Essential for taking the outer skin off of carrots and potatoes.

Garlic press: A good garlic press saves time while still allowing you the genuine pungency of fresh garlic.

Potato ricer: If you have a little extra space, this is the easiest way to get nice fluffy mashed potatoes and crisp hash browns.

Pots and pans, including a Dutch oven, 10- to 12-inch nonstick sauté pan, and large saucepan: It is possible to purchase myriad pots and pans, but these are the essentials in my kitchen.

Seasoned carbon-steel wok: I use this whenever I need to deep-fry anything. It efficiently uses oil, minimizes mess, and is easy to clean up.

Long-handled wood mixing spoons and spatulas: These are inexpensive and very helpful for cooking without scratching nonstick pans.

Silicone spatulas: I prefer these for scraping mixing bowls.

Thin metal spatulas: For pancakes and cookies, a thin metal spatula is the best way to release the bake.

Rimmed half-sheet baking pans: I have four of these, and I'm frequently glad to have that many, but really, two will do. For clarity: Full "sheet pans," also known as jelly-roll pans, are restaurant-sized

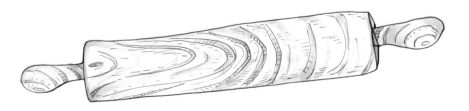

(approx. 18" x 26"); most home chefs will have half-sheet pans, which are approximately 12" x 18", or quarter-sheet pans (8¼" x 12½"). In this book, we'll use half-sheet pans and refer to them as such.

Baking tins, including round cake, 9x13-inch, 8-inch square, loaf, pie, tube, and cupcake: All useful in baking and with casseroles. I use both glass and metal vessels.

Cookie cutters: I have these in many shapes, but the ones I use most frequently are the plain 3-inch circles.

Bench scraper: I frequently use my bench scraper to release dough from the surface on which it was rolled. It's also helpful for transferring uncooked baked goods.

Marble slab: This is essential for making candy, and it provides a great surface for rolling dough.

Parchment paper: This provides a non-stick surface that is helpful in general baking and is critical for gluten-free baking.

Salad spinner: I love the way this tool so efficiently removes water from washed lettuce. I use this often because I prefer to purchase lettuce by the head rather than prewashed and torn.

Salt pig: Usually a small ceramic pot with a lid, it can be as ordinary as a repurposed yogurt container filled with salt. It's much easier to dip a measuring spoon into the salt than pouring it from a container, half into your measuring spoon—and half onto your stove.

Fat separator: A quart-sized fat separator is very useful when you make stock and want to use it right away rather than letting it cool to skim the fat off the top.

Storage vessels: I am a firm believer in the idea that the best way to conserve is to repurpose things that would otherwise be garbage. Most of my storage vessels are repurposed jars.

The Cast

Since you're taking the time to read this, and since most cookbooks are better with a few stories, I will introduce you to my cast here:

Me, Myself, and I—I am the author and developer of this cookbook, a mom, wife, sometime attorney, and creator.

Mr. Kent—My husband, whose face, stature, talent, and drive to fix things often leave people wondering if he really has superpowers. An adventurous eater, Mr. Kent is interested in many different foods and willing to try just about anything, which was one of the first things I found attractive about him.

Hervor—My eldest daughter, who has achieved the near impossible in going from disliking most of what I make for dinner to liking most of what I make for dinner. It has indeed been an epic journey. One might almost say a quest. Someday, perhaps, she will have her own quest, like the shieldmaiden that I have named her after here. She still doesn't like mushrooms.

Bear—My son, whose flexible approach to eating as a child was nearly derailed by a violent dislike of porridge and soup. However, Bear was persuaded to try peanut butter on the porridge and BBQ sauce in the soup, and now he is mostly resigned. Just don't expect him to do much with curry.

Nancy D—My second daughter, whose desire to help in the kitchen and enjoyment of vegetables rekindled my interest in cooking and faith in the process of making good food. Not only is she delighted to join me in concocting a batch of candy, but she loves to sneak bites of roasted broccoli and onions off the baking tray while I am plating dinner. Nancy D is detail-oriented and never forgets. Anything.

Dr. Lu—My youngest daughter, who would really rather be drawing and making up stories about her artwork than sitting at the table and eating anything that does not involve peanut butter or other snacks. We will keep the faith with her culinary development as we have with the others. And we will keep bringing her back to the table when she darts away.

Mom and Dad—My parents. They are wonderful. They helped start the Dinner Group (see next page), which was a pretty important part of my culinary development. They taught me and Kleine (see next page) about table manners and took us to lots of wonderful restaurants.

Mom 2 and Dad 2—My in-laws. They are wonderful, too. Mom 2 can make dinner at a moment's notice and never once has made me feel like my late-developing gluten issues are at all inconvenient.

Kleine—My younger sister. Talented and funny, Kleine was always willing to eat my creations when we were little girls. We have eaten an entire bag of pink-and-white circus animal cookies together, fought together, laughed together, and cried together. She is a good sister.

Grandma-Great—She really was a great grandma to many children over the years, and she was pretty wonderful, too. She spent forty years cooking three meals a day for the sheepherders in her family's sheep business, and she was the candy master in the family. Grandma-Great taught me a great deal about cooking and living. Grandma-Great passed away in November 2021, following the completion of writing this book.

Mimi—Mimi passed away fifteen years ago, but she also played a part in shaping my culinary experience. She taught me the value of sandwiches, pickles, chocolate angel food cake, and good grocery stores. I miss Mimi and her little yellow-and-white kitchen with its panoramic valley view and pot of bacon grease that was always ready for cooking my favorite cornmeal pancakes.

The Dinner Group—How can I describe the dinner group? Hilarious, sometimes irreverent, absolutely loyal, consistent. Mom and Dad established the group with three other couples before I was born. Over fifty years of dinner parties and many, many cookies, they have become family. After their kids grew up and moved into their own families, the Dinner Group has only become more active. They have explored the world together, laughed and eaten like they still enjoy life (they do), and mourned together. These are friendships to be envied.

So, there we are. Join us on this adventure in figuring out how to feed ourselves well and gracefully.

When I was a new mom with small children, people (usually women with grownup children) would tell me to savor the days—they would be over soon. I would smile and say something like, "Oh, yes, I'm trying to." And I'd cringe inside. When my children were small, time seemed to go so slowly. I loved spending my days with the littles, but sometimes the days were so long. I couldn't imagine what those experienced moms were talking about, and sometimes I wondered if I was missing an essential joy in my children. This thought would inevitably be followed by mom-guilt that tempted me to think that I just didn't love my kiddos enough.

Then Hervor began school, and the days had a new definition that they had lacked before. There were specified times for dropping off and picking up. We had more activities outside our little home universe. Time began slipping away more quickly. Fast-forward ten years, and all my children are in school. The weeks are so full of deadlines and activities that they fly by. Holidays and breaks come more and more rapidly. Milestones are encountered and passed with a speed that is increasingly alarming. I am beginning to see what those moms were talking about so many years ago, now that my oldest has entered secondary school and is a mere two years away from high school graduation! Life is undeniably very busy.

This collection of recipes is designed for those insane evenings when any dinner other than drive-through burgers and fries seems to be an impossibility. They can be on the table in about twenty to thirty minutes—so long as interruptions are kept at a minimum, of course!

The Essential Pantry

If you have these items on hand, you will be able to make the dinners in this section without a great deal of additional planning.

Shelf-Stable

Bacon bits
Boxed soup
Brown sugar
Chili
Cookies
Corn chips
Corn muffin mix
Croutons
English muffins
Mayonnaise
Mustard
Olive oil
Olives
Packaged mac & cheese
Pickles
Potato chips
Roasted almonds
Salt
Sandwich bread
Sour cherry jam
Water crackers

Perishable

Apples
Avocadoes
Butter
Carrots
Cheeses (cheddar, Parmesan, Monterey Jack, feta, sliced provolone)
Cucumbers
Deli ham
Deli turkey
Eggs
Grape tomatoes
Grapes
Green onions
Hummus
Limes
Milk
Oranges
Precooked bacon
Prewashed romaine lettuce
Ranch dressing
Salad kit
Salami
Smoked sausage
Sour cream

Frozen

Baguette
Petite peas

College-Style Dinners

QUICK ALTERNATIVES
20 to 35 Minutes Total

Corn Chips and Chili
with Vegetables and Dip

The first time I had this quick and easy dinner was at a Camp Fire day camp when I was seven or eight years old. We didn't bother with plates but just opened small bags of corn chips and poured the chili on top. I loved the crunchy-savory-saltiness of the whole thing. There was something so free and wonderful about this simple dinner in the woods.

Fast-forward several years, and now I'm the one ferrying kids to day camp and practices. On any given day, it seems that there is more to be done than time to do it. With everything there is to do in a day, sometimes I feel like I'm barely holding on to my dinner routine with my fingertips. I've learned that I need to dial back in the kitchen when life gets intense. I need to focus on ease and simplicity so instead of doing an hour of prep and another of cleanup, I can spend time doing the 50 million other things on my docket. In those moments, all I really need is corn chips and chili. A little cheese and green onion dress it up enough for dinner at a table with real utensils, but a disposable fork and a bag of chips work just fine in a pinch!

2 (9.25-ounce) bags corn chips 3 (14-ounce) cans chili 2 green onions 1 cup grated Mexican blend cheese ¼ cup sour cream	Place a handful of corn chips in individual soup bowls. (Try not to eat too many before dinner!) Heat the chili in a covered saucepan over medium heat. Slice the green onions into thin rings. Spoon the cheese, green onions, and sour cream in separate bowls.
2 medium carrots 1 small jicama	Peel and cut the carrots and jicama into sticks. Arrange on a plate.
1 lime, juiced 1 cup ranch dressing	In a serving dish, combine the lime juice and ranch dressing.
	When the chili is warm, spoon about ½ cup chili over the chips. Serve immediately with toppings and extra chips. Serve the vegetables and dip.

Gluten-Free Variation: Check to make sure to choose **gluten-free chili**. Lots of chilis are thickened with flour. **Corn chips** are generally gluten-free.

Mac and Cheese
with Candied Sausage and Green Peas

Boxed mac and cheese dinner is a childhood rite of passage, at least in America. When I was a child, it was an occasional treat that Mom left for me and Kleine to have when our babysitter made dinner, part of a rotation between boxed mac and cheese, frozen lasagna, and ramen noodles. No matter which babysitter dinner we had, frozen green peas were a constant accompaniment. Dad's business was frozen vegetables, so we ate a lot of petite green peas. It definitely left an imprint on my taste preferences. To this day I want green peas with my pasta. Childhood traditions are powerful, but the sweetness of peas with the savory pasta is something you should try.

Mac and cheese is good, but after a while . . . well, I just didn't love it *that* much. Enter candied sausage. Like a bit of gilt on a plain old teapot, candied sausage elevated plain old mac and cheese to a new level. There was a textural interplay between the creamy, soft noodles and the robust sausage with its salty-sweet crispiness that made the whole dinner feel more like real food. This makes a decent dinner when you're short on time. And I have never had a child turn down mac and cheese—although some ask that the sausage be put on the side.

1 (16-ounce) package frozen petite green peas	Set frozen green peas in a saucepan and barely cover with warm water.
Water 1 teaspoon salt	Add salt to a large saucepan ⅔ full of water, and bring it to a rolling boil.
12–16 ounces smoked sausage 1 tablespoon olive oil 2 teaspoons brown sugar	Slice sausage lengthwise and then into ½-inch semicircles. Place a large sauté pan over medium heat and add the oil when the pan is warm. Sauté the sausage, stirring frequently, until it is speckled with brown spots. Add the brown sugar and cook, stirring frequently, until the sugar melts onto the sausage. Remove from heat.
2 (7.5-ounce) boxes macaroni and cheese dinner	Once the water comes to a boil, add the pasta and cook for about 5 minutes. Test a piece to see if it is a good consistency. Cook a little longer if you like it more tender.
	While the macaroni is cooking, turn the heat on the peas to high. Allow them to come to a simmer, then remove from heat.
⅓ cup butter, softened ¾ cup milk Boxed macaroni and cheese flavor packets 1 (6.6-ounce) package goldfish crackers, for garnish	Drain the pasta and do not rinse. Return pasta to the pan. Stir in the butter then the milk and the contents of the cheese packets until smooth. Stir in the sausage. Garnish with goldfish crackers. Serve immediately with the peas.

Gluten-Free Variation: Use **gluten-free macaroni and cheese dinner** instead of the regular mac and cheese. Make sure to use **gluten-free sausage**.

Supermarket Small Bites
(Or, a Great Picnic)

I remember the first time I really appreciated the magic and hilarity of a Shakespearean comedy. I was fifteen and spent the night with my cousin at her cute college house while my mom attended a conference. We watched Kenneth Branagh's *Much Ado about Nothing*. I was swept into this world of ochre buildings, crunching gravel courtyards, glossy green vineyards, and frothy white summer dresses. I wanted to be there with them, especially at their picnic in the opening scene. Beatrice ate luscious purple grapes and sang "Sigh no more, ladies, sigh no more" as the brave warriors galloped toward them across the gorgeous

Italian countryside. That scene elevated my idea of the ideal picnic and, though none of my picnics have yet come close to that sheer gorgeousness, the charm of eating alfresco continues to beckon me outside for dinner.

This recipe makes a fun picnic in the summertime and is an easy last-minute dinner anytime. Let kids pick their favorite cheeses, crackers, and fruit to help them get involved and interested. You are mere steps away from your own idyll, at least until the water gets spilled on the crackers, or the cat sidles through the picnic and runs off with the cheese.

1 (10-ounce) carton hummus 2 tablespoons olive oil ¼ teaspoon coarse salt 1 wedge soft cheese (such as Camembert) 1 wedge medium cheese (such as Gouda) 20 slices salami 10 slices deli turkey	Spoon the hummus into a bowl, drizzle with olive oil, and sprinkle with salt. Arrange the cheeses on a plate and let them sit at room temperature while you prepare everything else. Arrange salami and turkey on a plate and refrigerate.
1 cucumber 1 cup grape tomatoes 2-3 carrots 2 apples or 1 bunch grapes	Cut the cucumber in half lengthwise, then cut each half into half-moon slices. Wash the grape tomatoes. Peel the carrots and cut into approximately 3-inch sticks. Arrange the vegetables on a plate. Slice the apples if using. Arrange the apples or grapes on a plate.
1 baguette 1 package water crackers	Cut the baguette into slanted 1-inch thick slices. Arrange the baguette slices and crackers on a plate.
½ cup roasted salted almonds ¼ cup sour cherry jam ½ cup pickles of your choice ½ cup olives of your choice	Place almonds, jam, pickles, and olives in dishes and arrange on the table with the proteins, fruits, vegetables, bread, and crackers.
Favorite store-bought cookies	Serve at the end of the picnic!

Gluten-Free Variation: Cut 8 slices of **gluten-free bread** in half and toast them until the tops are just crisp and beginning to look toasty. Gently scrape the bread with a peeled **garlic clove**. Lightly brush with **extra-virgin olive oil** and sprinkle with coarse **salt**. Keep warm. Arrange **gluten-free rice crackers** on a plate to serve. Prepare and arrange all other ingredients as mentioned. Choose **gluten-free cookies** to end the dinner.

Club Sandwiches with Potato Chips

Sandwiches always remind me of my grand-mothers. When I eat them, nostalgic memories of lunch dates with Mimi and Grandma-Great begin to bubble up in my mind: sometimes in a sunny white kitchen with homemade sandwiches on toasted bread, sometimes at a lunch counter downtown, where I had to eat a sandwich before I could order an ice cream sundae. In these rosy memories are my grandmothers as I love to re-member them: stately ladies with "set" hair and ready smiles who thought I was the most amaz-ing person in the world—at least, that's how they made me feel. I expect that it is also how they made each of my nineteen cousins and my sister feel as well. Grandmothers are special.

Mimi, my paternal grandmother, loved corned beef sandwiches. Grandma-Great, my maternal grandmother, was most happy with a lamb sandwich. As a child, I preferred cheese-burgers or Mimi's peanut butter and jam sand-wiches, both sides of the bread buttered before the jam and peanut butter were spread (don't judge, they're amazing). As I grew older, I began to appreciate more sophisticated sandwiches, like the club. This sandwich is much bolder and more substantial than a PB&J—even with the butter layer. I love how the salty meat, smoky bacon, and buttery bread provide the counterpoint to creamy cheese, mayo, and tomato. This is a sandwich that can stand fully in dinner territory. Let kids make their own sandwiches to engage them more fully in the meal, and make sure to tell them your own grandma stories!

1 (2.5-ounce) package precooked bacon	Heat bacon according to package instructions.
2 Roma tomatoes 6 lettuce leaves 1 avocado	Slice the tomatoes thinly. Separate, wash, and dry the lettuce. Slice the avocado thinly.
1 loaf sliced French or sourdough bread	Lightly toast bread slices.
Soft butter Mayonnaise Mustard 6 slices provolone cheese 8 ounces sliced ham 6 slices Swiss cheese 8 ounces sliced smoked turkey	Spread a thin layer of butter on two slices of lightly toasted bread. Add a light layer of mayonnaise and mustard. Layer provolone cheese, ham, tomato, avocado, Swiss cheese, turkey, bacon, and lettuce. Top with the remaining slice of bread. Cut diagonally in quarters. Repeat as necessary to get the number of sandwiches you need.
Potato chips	Serve sandwiches with potato chips.

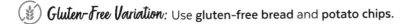 **Gluten-Free Variation:** Use **gluten-free bread** and **potato chips**.

Chicken in the Park
with Deli Sides, Chips, and Cookies

When my children were still very little, and it became clear that feeding them was going to get challenging, my pediatrician gave me some advice about dinner. He told me that some days would be tough as Hervor, Bear, Nancy D, and Dr. Lu figured out their worlds. He recommended that dinner on those days might be best served by picking up some fried chicken and heading to the park for an impromptu picnic. An unplanned picnic can shake things up enough and wear kids out enough

that the troubles of the afternoon float away in the fresh air of the evening. After a picnic in the park, everyone can return home fed and tired for bed, with little or no mess to clean up. Indeed, there are days when this is really the best option for dinner.

By adding a few deli sides, and perhaps some chips and cookies, you can have a feast at the park. Make sure to pick your favorite cookies for a little self-care. Maybe some good chocolate too.

Deli fried chicken	Order enough for your family's needs.
Deli side salads	Choose your favorite. Don't forget napkins (maybe pick up some wipes) and utensils.
Grapes, cherries, or apples	Choose your favorite (ideally in-season) fruit.
Chips	A multipack of small chip bags may be the quickest way to peace.
Cookies	Again, choose your favorite.
Water	Don't forget to purchase water bottles if you forgot to bring eco-friendly ones from home in the mad dash to get everyone out the door and in the car.

Gluten-Free Variation: Sadly, unless you are incredibly lucky to live near a specialty restaurant that makes **gluten-free fried chicken**, fried chicken will not be gluten-free. You could choose **rotisserie chicken** instead (check the label for gluten warnings). Choose **gluten-free deli sides**, **chips**, and **cookies**.

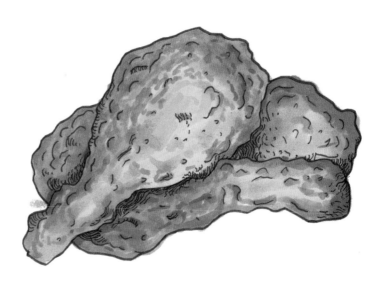

Cheesy Scrambled Eggs with Fruit, Bacon, Pickles, and English Muffins

I credit my college roommate Cheri with this recipe. Cher hailed from the great state of Wisconsin and appreciated good cheddar. Prior to sharing a kitchen with her, I had never thought of putting cheese in scrambled eggs—mainly because I'd had a bad experience once at an all-night diner where the scrambled eggs arrived with a half-melted slice of processed cheese on top. That was definitely not appealing. I soon learned that Cher's eggs were a different story. Silky and just cheesy enough, these eggs are definitely satisfying enough for dinner. Many years later, I learned that Cher's technique of adding the cheese near the end of the cooking process was similar to a classic French technique that Julia Child was taught at Le Cordon Bleu in the 1950s. I love finding similarities in cooking across time and borders!

1 large bunch red seedless grapes 2 medium oranges	Preheat the oven to 170 degrees F. Wash grapes and cut into small bunches. Slice oranges into sections. Arrange the oranges and grapes on a plate.
1 (2.5-ounce) package precooked bacon	Heat according to package instructions.
Pickles, sweet or dill as you prefer	Arrange several pickles in a dish.
1 (6-ounce) package English muffins Butter	Slice the muffins, then toast to your desired crispiness and butter them. Place toasted muffins in the warm oven.
8 eggs ¼ cup milk or cream ¼ teaspoon salt 2 tablespoons butter ½ cup shredded sharp cheddar cheese	Gently whisk together the eggs with the milk and salt. Place a nonstick frying pan over medium-low heat. When you can feel heat through the pan, add butter to the pan and swirl it around as it melts. Pour the egg mixture into the pan and let cook for 30 seconds. Scrape the sides and bottom of the pan with a spatula every 30 seconds or so until the eggs are almost completely cooked but still soft. Reduce the heat to low and gently stir in the cheese until it melts. Remove from the heat.
Jam	Serve eggs, pickles, fruit, bacon, and English muffins with jam at the table.

Gluten-Free Variation: Use gluten-free **English muffins** or **bread**.

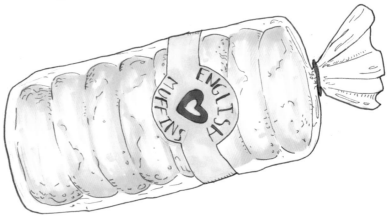

Deli Soup with Cornbread and Green Salad

When I met a certain tall, dark, and handsome graduate student during my final year of law school, I decided I just had to make time for him, though my spare time was limited. Mr. Kent and I packed dates in between study sessions, classes, projects, exams, and commutes. Once he surprised me with cookies in the library, although he accidently tripped the fire alarm in the process. One evening, I made dinner for us by bringing crackers and canned clam chowder that I heated in the school break room's microwave. It was a funny little meal—the food wasn't particularly remarkable—but I found it to be just as homey and romantic as dinner with a newly discovered true love should be. The food didn't particularly matter—rather, it was the company and the time we took with one another that made it special.

Now that we find ourselves in the wonderful and hectic life we have created together, a quick soup dinner with almost no prep can be just what we need at the end of a busy day. And if some of my children (Bear and Dr. Lu) have to be convinced I'm not trying to secretly poison them with the soup, well, I suppose that gives us another opportunity to work on our negotiation skills. Let kids choose the soup and help with the cornbread. This is a great dinner to make after a day of skiing in the winter or a cool afternoon walk on a hazy October day.

2 (8.5-ounce) packages corn muffin mix

2 eggs

⅔ cup milk

Butter or nonstick cooking spray

Preheat the oven to 400 degrees F. Mix the muffins according to package instructions. Grease a standard 12-cup muffin tin or a 12-inch ovenproof skillet. Pour batter into prepared pan. Bake muffins for 12–15 minutes or skillet bread for 18–20 minutes until the tops are set and the edges begin to look toasty.

---

1 (32-ounce) container supermarket deli soup of choice

Place soup in a medium saucepan over low heat, covered, to keep warm.

---

1 salad kit of choice

While the cornbread is baking, layer the salad ingredients in a bowl and set aside. Dress the salad immediately prior to serving.

Gluten-Free Variation: Use **gluten-free boxed or canned soup** instead of deli soup. Use **gluten-free cornbread mix** and **salad kit**.

When I brought Hervor into this world, I had no idea what was ahead of me. I was going forward with blind faith, a little apprehension, and undeniable excitement for the adventure ahead. Those first few years of being a mom were a new adventure that was full of discoveries, joys, some frustrations, and such sweetness. My world was still very small.

As I welcomed three more humans into this world, and as they began to grow up and develop more complex personalities, life became significantly more complicated. Evening activities encroached on dinnertime. Bouts of my own discouragement made mountains out of the molehill of dinner preparation. Textures and flavors became an issue with young palates. I gradually realized that I had come to see dinner as another chore to be finished, like laundry and bathroom cleaning, rather than as an opportunity for creativity. I felt like my creative juices were being sapped by my perpetually unfinished to-do list and too much complaining—and I hated it.

So I started to fight back. I began by winnowing out the things that are really important to me and let the chaff of others' expectations fall away. I keep working at this with each new fold in my life. Sometimes I don't feel guilty about not doing everything—although I often do—but as I reassess my expectations of myself and work to set and keep boundaries, an amazing thing happens. I feel more like the self I like to be around. I celebrate my successes without dragging them down with any accompanying failures. If Bear eats his bowl of curry without complaining, I smile, even if he picked out all the zucchini. Baby steps have become acceptable to me, and, while my standards have not necessarily changed, my understanding of how they will eventually be met has.

This section is where you will find dinners that are easy and relatively quick to make. These dinners are not particularly broadening, and many could be considered quick-to-the-table comfort food. There are seasons when we want chef-worthy escapades in the kitchen, and there are seasons for just keeping it simple. Knowing where you are is a huge portion of the battle.

Quick-Prep Dinners

AKA THE MOM-CHEF'S HANDBOOK
35 to 70 Minutes Total

Pasta alla Carbonara with Green Peas

A few years ago, at the end of a long, dreary, snowy winter, when I was more than ready for the air to grow warm and the daffodils to push up through the damp earth, I read *The Enchanted April* by Elizabeth von Arnim. I was transported to Italy with Lotty and Rose, to sunshine and warmth at the iconic castle above the sea. It is a book worth reading if you have not done so, especially if you happen to be experiencing the sort of winter that lags on well into March. Mrs. Fisher, the Victorian caricature in the novel, humorously struggled with Italy's long pasta noodles: "It was very well cooked, but Mrs. Fisher had never cared for macaroni, especially not this long, worm-shaped variety. She found it difficult to eat,—slippery, wriggling off her fork, making her look, she felt, undignified when, having got it as she supposed into her mouth, ends of it yet hung out" (von Armin, *The Enchanted April* [New York: Doubleday, 1923], 120).

Mrs. Fisher might prefer this dish made with bite-sized noodles such as penne or orecchiette. Pasta alla carbonara is a special treat from Italy that is easily translated to the average kitchen manned by the average cook. There are just a few details that will make this dish great. Keep everything warm or hot before mixing together, and serve the pasta as quickly as you can after you put it all together.

1 tablespoon olive oil 1 medium onion ½ teaspoon salt 6-8 ounces pancetta or bacon, chopped	Place the olive oil in a large Dutch oven over medium heat. Cut the onion into ¼-inch dice and sauté with the salt until the onion becomes translucent. Add the pancetta and cook for about 8 minutes, stirring frequently, until the fat is rendered. Remove to a paper towel–lined plate to drain. Place the onion and pancetta mixture in a bowl and cover to keep warm. Wipe the Dutch oven clean. Fill with water and set over high heat.
1 (16-ounce) package frozen petite green peas	Place in a small saucepan and just cover with warm water.
4 eggs	Whisk thoroughly with ¼-cup pasta water (see instruction below).
1 tablespoon salt 1 (16-ounce) package ribbon pasta (such as linguine, fettuccine, or pappardelle) of choice	Add salt to the water in the Dutch oven. Add the pasta and cook according to package instructions. After the pasta has cooked for five minutes, ladle approximately ¼ cup of the pasta water and trickle the water into the eggs while whisking them. Turn the peas on high and cook until they just come to a simmer, then remove them from the heat.
2 cups finely shredded Parmesan cheese, room temperature	Stir the cheese into the eggs. Turn off the stove. Drain the pasta but do not rinse. Immediately return the pasta to the Dutch oven and pour the egg mixture on top, stirring constantly off the heat, until the eggs thicken and form a sauce on the pasta. Continue stirring and tossing the pasta for another minute or two to prevent the eggs from curdling. If the sauce fails to thicken, return the pot to very low heat and stir constantly. Once it thickens, stir in the onion and pancetta mixture. Season with salt and fresh pepper if desired. Serve immediately with the peas.

(⚘) *Gluten-Free Variation:* Use **gluten-free pasta.** Small shapes, such as penne, work better than long noodles, such as spaghetti, which tend to break as they are tossed.

Pancakes
with Homemade Syrup and Smoky Carrots

I was a strange little girl in that I disliked just about any breakfast other than cold cereal—including pancakes and eggs and waffles. There was something about how they got mushy when the syrup soaked into the pancake that I just did not like. That is the most significant childhood texture issue that I can remember! Thankfully, my mom kept trying, and I eventually came to understand the allure of good breakfast food. It likely helped that Grandma-Great made hearty sourdough pancakes and Mimi made delicate, sweet and crisp cornmeal pancakes. I began to see that even Mom's biscuit-mix pancakes were pretty wonderful, and I came around. I'm still a little snobby about preferring to eat the pancakes right off the griddle when they are at the peak of their toasty tenderness. Happily, since I am the primary pancake maker, I can accommodate this little whim.

Thankfully, Hervor, Bear, Nancy D, and Dr. Lu all seem to like breakfast foods pretty well, so pancakes for dinner are a fun treat that they enjoy. This is a great option for dinner when you haven't been to the grocery store for a while, or when you're just returning home from out of town right at dinnertime. While it does create quite a few dishes, it can be on the table quickly and can be made from ingredients you usually have on hand.

3 large carrots, peeled ¼ cup olive oil ¼ teaspoon salt 1 teaspoon brown sugar ¼ teaspoon smoked paprika	Cut the carrots into sticks. Place in medium saucepot and add remaining ingredients. Bring to a simmer over medium-high heat. Reduce the heat to medium-low, cover, and cook for 15 minutes until the carrots are tender. Check seasonings and keep warm.

Pancakes

3 cups/425 grams flour 2 teaspoons baking powder 1 teaspoon baking soda 1 teaspoon salt 1 cup plain yogurt 1½ cups milk 2 eggs ⅓ cup oil ¼ cup sugar	Whisk dry ingredients together in a large bowl. Whisk the wet ingredients into the dry ingredients until just combined. The batter will remain a bit lumpy. Allow it to sit and get fluffy while you make the syrup and preheat the frying pan or griddle over medium heat.

Syrup

1 cup water 2 cups sugar ¼ cup brown sugar 1 pinch salt 2 teaspoons maple flavoring 1 teaspoon vanilla	Pour water into a 4-cup microwave-safe measuring cup. Microwave for three minutes. Stir in sugars and salt. Microwave an additional three minutes, stir, then microwave two minutes, stir, then microwave one minute. The syrup should be thickened but not as thick as store-bought maple-flavored syrup. Stir in flavorings.

Suggested condiments

Softened butter Peanut butter or other nut butter Fruit	Preheat the griddle or sauté pan over medium heat. Make 3-inch pancakes by pouring ⅛ cup batter in pools on hot griddle. Flip the pancakes when they are puffed and there are several bubbles on the surface. Serve hot with syrup and condiments of your choice.

🌾 *Gluten-Free Variation:* Whisk together 3 cups/425 grams **gluten-free flour blend**, 2 teaspoons **baking powder**, 1 teaspoon **baking soda**, 1 teaspoon **salt**, ¼ teaspoon **xanthan gum** (omit if your flour blend contains xanthan gum), and ¼ cup **sugar**. In a separate bowl, whisk together 1½ cups **milk**, 1 cup **Greek yogurt**, 2 **eggs**, and ⅓ cup **oil**. Whisk together and allow mixture to stand for 3–4 minutes. Cook as directed above.

Toothpick Dinner with Sausage, Roasted Potatoes and Onions, Tomatoes and Feta, and Salted Caramel Apple Slices

When I was a little girl in the 1980s, I remember watching my parents get ready for their dinners out with the Dinner Group. Inspired by America's gourmet renaissance of the 1970s, they and a group of friends decided to get together monthly to have a very sophisticated potluck dinner. They nearly always dressed up, the men in sport coats and ties and the women in chic dresses or pantsuits. The hostess would provide the main course, and the visiting couples would be assigned to appetizers, salads, or desserts. When Mom hosted, we carefully laid the table with white linens, her wedding china, crystal drinkware, silver tableware, and beautiful flower centerpieces. At

Christmastime, the children were invited for a great dinner and gift exchange. My favorite part of these dinners—besides the epic cookie platters that accompanied the gift exchange—was always the appetizers.

This toothpick dinner is almost as fun to eat as those wonderful appetizers were. It's hearty and savory with a sweet touch in the caramel apples. Toothpicks make everything seem a little more like a party—even without getting dressed up. This is based on the sheet-pan dinner concept. Sheet-pan dinners are popular for a very good reason. They are extraordinarily simple and do not produce too many dishes for washing up!

4–5 medium Yukon Gold potatoes, peeled ¼ cup olive oil ½ teaspoon salt	Preheat the oven to 425 degrees F. Cut the potatoes into ½-inch chunks. Place on a half-sheet pan, drizzle with oil, and sprinkle with salt. Make sure the potatoes are not touching too much. Roast in the oven about 15 minutes, remove from the oven, flip the potatoes over with a spatula, and roast in the oven an additional 15 minutes, until the potatoes are soft on the inside and crispy outside.
1 (12- to 16-ounce) Polish sausage 1 medium onion 2 tablespoons olive oil ½ teaspoon salt	Cut the sausage in half lengthwise, then into ½-inch-thick slices. Cut the onion into 1-inch slices. Place on a second half-sheet pan. Toss with oil and sprinkle with salt. When you take the potatoes out after their first 15 minutes, put the sausage and onion pan in the oven too. Roast for the final 15 minutes.
1 (8- to 10-ounce) block feta cheese, preferably brined 8 ounces grape or cherry tomatoes 2 tablespoons pesto 1 tablespoon mayonnaise 1 teaspoon lemon juice 1 pinch sea salt	While the potatoes are roasting, cut the feta into cubes a little smaller than the tomatoes. Arrange the tomatoes and feta on a plate. This is the place for a fun contrasting design! Whisk together pesto, mayonnaise, lemon juice, and salt. Serve in a small bowl as a dip for the tomatoes and feta.
2 medium sweet-tart apples, such as Pink Lady ⅓ cup salted caramel sauce	Slice the apples ¼-inch thick and place on serving plate. Drizzle the caramel over the apples.
Box of round toothpicks	Serve dinner with toothpicks for spearing the food.

 **Gluten-Free Variation:** Use **gluten-free sausage** and **caramel sauce**.

Lox and Cream Cheese Bagels
with Classic Caesar Salad

I have visited New York City twice and do not really remember having a bagel experience either time. Sad, perhaps? But that pastrami sandwich I ate was memorable in its three-inch-thick massiveness. And the Caesar salad, with its croutons made of thick slices of baguette, was also something I thought about for a long time. Later, despite my missed opportunity with New York bagels, I discovered this classic at a local bagel shop: lox and cream cheese bagels. I love the creamy cheese juxtaposed with the salty, rich cold smoked salmon. The capers and thinly sliced red onions on top were piquant and crunchy and, as

such, the perfect counterpoint to the rich bed on which they lay. Maybe it would have been better in New York, but I was hooked on lox and bagels out West.

I have served this dinner in a bar format. My kids love having some control over their dinners and seem to be more willing to try things like capers when they are optional. It also takes some pressure off the cook in that last frenzied minute of getting dinner on plates and on the table. Once there, the bar style of service also makes it necessary to learn to pass the food and listen to your tablemates. Manners!

½ baguette	Preheat the oven to 350 degrees F. Cut the baguette into 1-inch-thick slices and then quarter them. Spread the bread cubes on a baking sheet. Bake for 20 minutes.
Dressing ⅓ cup extra-virgin olive oil 2 tablespoons fresh lemon juice 1 tablespoon mayonnaise 1 large clove garlic, pressed ¼ teaspoon salt ⅛ teaspoon freshly ground pepper	Whisk together, then taste to adjust seasonings.
2 hearts romaine lettuce ½ cup grated Parmesan cheese	Wash and dry the romaine. Layer Parmesan on the bottom of a large serving bowl and top with lettuce. Keep cool.
4–6 ounces sliced cold-smoked salmon ¼ cup capers ½ red onion, sliced very thin	Arrange on serving dishes in the center of the table.
2 tablespoons butter 2 tablespoons olive oil ½ teaspoon garlic salt	Heat a sauté pan over medium heat and add the butter and olive oil. Stir together as the butter melts. Add the bread cubes and cook, stirring occasionally, until the cubes absorb the fat and become toasty and crisp on the outside. Sprinkle the croutons with garlic salt and allow them to cool in the pan.
6 large bagels (plain or everything) 8 ounces plain cream cheese	Toast the bagels, either in the toaster or by placing them in a single layer on a rimmed half-sheet pan under the oven broiler for a minute or so (watch carefully!). Toss the salad with the dressing, checking to make sure the seasonings are right. Place two halves of a bagel on each plate and spread with cream cheese. Serve immediately. Diners will add their desired toppings at the table.

Gluten-Free Variation: Use **gluten-free bagels**. Use **gluten-free bread** for croutons.

Vegetable Stew That Even My Kids Like with Blue Corn Tortilla Chips and Poached Egg

The first recipe I ever published was for a vegetable soup like this one. It had a distinguished place in my junior high school newspaper and was my mom's recipe that used tomato juice in the stock. My mom helped me write it, and I was really excited to submit it and see it in print, even if it was only the photocopied school paper. Small achievements! At that point, I don't think that I had any inkling of how much time I would spend in recipe development a few years hence. I hadn't heard of zoology then either, and I had never even considered law school. I was just a junior high student trying to understand how I fit into the sea of bewildering quasi-maturity in which I was swimming.

This is really a winter vegetable soup, since parsnips are difficult to obtain in the summer. If you are making it in the summer, you can substitute new potatoes, zucchini, summer squash, tomatoes, and green beans for the potatoes, parsnips, carrots, and celery. If you are lucky enough to live near a farmers market and can fit in a visit, go there for inspiration!

2 tablespoons olive oil

1 large onion, diced

½ teaspoon salt

4 large cloves garlic, pressed

Place a large Dutch oven over medium-low heat and add the olive oil. When hot, add the onion and salt and sauté, stirring frequently, until the onion is fragrant and translucent, about 5 minutes. Stir in the garlic and cook for 30 seconds while stirring constantly.

1 (32-ounce) carton vegetable stock

1 teaspoon mixed dried herb blend

1 bay leaf

1 tablespoon tomato paste

Pour the stock into the onion mixture and scrape the bottom of the pan to remove any browned bits. Stir in the herbs, bay leaf, and tomato paste. Turn the heat to low.

4 medium Yukon Gold potatoes, peeled

1 small sweet potato, peeled

2 parsnips, peeled

3 carrots, peeled

3 ribs celery

4 cups water

Cut the potatoes, sweet potato, and parsnips into ½-inch dice and add to the broth. Cut the carrots and celery into ¼-inch dice and add to the soup. Simmer for 30 minutes or until the potato is tender and the soup thickens slightly. Remove the bay leaf. Taste to check seasonings; add additional salt in ¼-teaspoon increments if necessary.

6–8 eggs

1 tablespoon distilled white vinegar

Coarse salt

1 bunch parsley, chopped with stems

Blue corn tortilla chips

Fill a shallow pan with water, add the vinegar, and bring to a simmer (a few bubbles breaking the surface). Ladle stew into bowls. Crack and slide eggs one by one into the simmering water. Cook for 2–3 minutes, or until the white is set and the yolk is still soft. Remove the eggs individually with a slotted spoon, floating one or two on top of each bowl of stew. Sprinkle a little coarse salt on top of the eggs. Sprinkle stew liberally with parsley and serve with tortilla chips.

Gluten-Free Variation: This menu is naturally gluten-free.

Asian-Style Chicken Salad Bar
with Steamed Rice

I really started feeling independent when I began going out to dinner with friends and without my parents. I was driving a car they provided, with gas they paid for, and I was using the $20 my mom gave me before I left, but somehow all of that seemed completely peripheral, and I felt like I was really grown up. This was at a moment when gourmet burger restaurants were offering truly mountainous salads as a "healthy" alternative to burgers and fries. Exposé nutritional analyses revealed that these salads were nearly as calorie dense as the hamburgers, but by that time, they had found their own permanent places on the menus. One of the most popular of these was usually called "Chinese chicken salad." The creamy and slightly tangy dressing plays nicely with tender chicken, crunchy chow mein noodles and almonds, and sweet fruit. Although there is nothing particularly innovative or authentic about that salad, its qualities absolutely justified its popularity.

Here I've separated the components into a bar format, which is generally more appealing to my kiddos than a mixed salad. With a salad bar, each diner is empowered to make choices about toppings and whether or not to let the components touch each other. While salad may never have the appeal of tacos, allowing kids to make their own salads can make salad night almost as cool as a taco bar.

4–5 boneless skinless chicken thighs 1 teaspoon salt	(*Optional–this extra step is worth it if you plan ahead.*) Place chicken on a plate and sprinkle with salt. Cover and place in the refrigerator for 1 to 24 hours.
1½ cups (or 2 rice cooker cups) jasmine or sushi rice	Cook the rice according to package instructions.
4 cups water 1 bay leaf	Add the thighs to a saucepan and cover with water. Turn the heat to high and heat until the water begins to simmer. Reduce the heat to medium-low and simmer for 4 minutes. Remove from the heat and cover for ½ hour. Remove the chicken from the water and allow it to rest for 5 minutes. Roughly chop the chicken.
Dressing ¼ cup mayonnaise ¼ cup plain yogurt 2 tablespoons vegetable oil 1 tablespoon rice vinegar 1 tablespoon prepared mustard ¼ cup sugar 1½ teaspoons poppy seeds ½ teaspoon salt	Whisk together to combine. Taste and adjust the seasonings. Place in a small pitcher or mug, then set aside.
1 head romaine lettuce	Wash, dry, and tear into pieces. Place in a bowl and keep cool.
1 tablespoon butter 1 cup toasted sliced almonds 2 tablespoons sugar 1 tablespoon water ½ teaspoon Chinese five-spice seasoning ⅛ teaspoon salt	Add butter to a sauté pan over medium heat. After the butter melts, add the remaining ingredients. Sauté until the sugar melts and the almonds turn golden brown. Remove from the heat and spread almonds on a plate. Allow the almonds to cool and then place them in a small bowl. >

Asian-Style Chicken Salad Bar with Steamed Rice

½ pineapple, cut into ½-inch pieces

2 cups chow mein noodles

2 green onions, chopped

1 cup dried sweetened cranberries

Arrange on the table in separate bowls alongside the dressing and (optional) chicken so everyone can make their own salads with rice on the side.

Gluten-Free Variation: Instead of the chow mein noodles, use **corn tortilla strips**. Cut 3 **corn tortillas** into ⅛-inch thick strips. Heat ⅓ cup **oil** in a small saucepan. When the oil begins to look like it is moving, drop one strip into the oil. If it bubbles, put in a handful of tortilla strips. Fry, stirring every 30 seconds, until the strips become crisp and golden brown. Remove to a paper towel–lined plate to drain, then sprinkle with salt.

Table Talk

One way to keep everyone at the table and eating is to make sure interesting conversations happen while everyone is there. Some families have conversation starter jars, while others exchange bits of a story for bites eaten. Tablemates can be encouraged to talk about things they found interesting in a day or to bring jokes to share. One family patriarch expected his children to bring to the table stories of some good deed that they had done during the day. Table talk can be very illuminating and can encourage people to remain even after the food is gone. It's good to be together; the nourishment of spirits is at least as important as the nourishment of bodies. Lots of word games, such as Twenty Questions or "I'm going on a picnic . . ." can be found on the internet—or remembered from childhood. These all serve to improve the conversation flow. Here are some of my family's favorites:

1. *Twenty Questions:* Categories like geography, science, literature, and current events are fun.
2. *The Picnic Game:* One person comes up with a pattern, such as "I'm going on a picnic, and I'm bringing an Apple, a Bike, and Chips," and uses the pattern to dictate whether other participants can come on the picnic. As players pick up on the pattern, they're allowed to come and bring the items they propose.
3. *Choose Your Own Adventure:* One person starts a story and other tablemates add to it or one person tells a story with periodic stops for the other participants to choose which course the protagonist will take.

"Hawaiian" Haystacks
with Orange Tofu

I had never heard of "Hawaiian" haystacks before becoming a college student and beginning to eat Sunday dinners with my roommates. After having them once, I began to notice them everywhere. I could see their potential; however, I wasn't sold on the gloppy cream-of-chicken gravy that was served with the other toppings. Teriyaki sauce seems like a much better topping to me; although, if you have real leftover gravy, it would probably be excellent as well.

Hawaiian haystacks fall firmly into the category of dishes that are named "Hawaiian" because they include pineapple—regardless of any actual connection to Hawaii. Despite the dubious nomenclature, this bar-style dinner is always popular with my children. The salty sweetness of the tofu is a great counterpoint for creamy, acidic, sweet, and crunchy toppings. Chow mein noodles are entirely optional.

2¼ cups sushi rice (or 3 rice cooker cups)	Cook rice in rice cooker or according to package instructions.
2 (14-ounce) packages firm tofu 1½ teaspoons salt	Cut tofu into 1-inch cubes. Place on an absorbent towel and sprinkle with salt. Allow the tofu to sit for 30 minutes. Preheat the oven to 425 degrees F. Place tofu in a single layer in a 9x13-inch pan.
Orange sauce 3 tablespoons orange juice concentrate, thawed ⅓ cup soy sauce 1 teaspoon rice vinegar 2 teaspoons cornstarch ¼ cup brown sugar	Whisk together and pour over the tofu. Place pan into the preheated oven. Bake for 15 minutes, stir gently, then bake for an additional 15 minutes.
1 cup grated cheddar cheese 1 bell pepper, diced 1 cup grape tomatoes, quartered 1 cup pineapple chunks 1 cup roasted and salted coconut chips 3 green onions, chopped Furikake seasoning Soy sauce	Arrange the toppings in small bowls on the table. Serve by placing a bed of rice on the plate, then spoon the tofu over the rice. Serve at the table so diners can add as many of the toppings and sauce as they would like.

Gluten-Free Variation: Make sure that the **soy sauce** and **furikake** are gluten-free.

As a little girl, I loved the Ramona books by Beverly Cleary. Ramona was such a relatable character for me because she made mistakes and sometimes didn't understand everything that was going on. I loved the books. Then, in 1988, PBS broadcast a miniseries that was so true to the books, honestly, it gave me unrealistic expectations about what to expect from dramatizations of literature ever after. More's the pity. One of the most vivid of these episodes involved a slow cooker. Ramona's family came home late after a long day of school and work, and they were hungrily anticipating a stew that had been cooking all day in the slow cooker. Unfortunately, the slow cooker had not been plugged in, and the stew was raw and cold. The girls witnessed a big parent fight and subsequently worried about their parents' marriage. There is a great dream sequence in the miniseries where Ramona's mom throws the slow cooker away. But after a good night's sleep, everyone was ready to forgive and forget, and the slow cooker remained in the kitchen.

I have had a few "un-plugged-in slow cooker" experiences of my own, and they are immensely frustrating, but, for the most part, the slow cooker is a really useful appliance. When I get a slow cooker dinner started—and plugged in—early in the day, I feel like I have given myself a leg up on a busy evening. It's lovely to come home with a hungry crew to find that dinner is mostly finished. Here are some recipes to enjoy—and add to. Just remember to plug in the slow cooker!

Slow-Cooker Dinners

FOR WHEN YOU'RE COMING IN HOT OR EXHAUSTED
30 to 60 Minutes Prep

Slow-Cooker Strata
with Green Salad

When I was a little girl, one of my mom's signature dishes was her breakfast casserole. I would get so excited when she began making it for two reasons: (1) I loved eating it, especially the cheesy, eggy, mushroomy bites, and (2) the recipe required crustless white bread. Mom would buy a loaf of the springy white bread that was never otherwise seen in our whole-wheat household, and she would cut the crusts off before cubing the bread. My sister and I gorged ourselves on those crusts. Now, Hervor, Nancy D, and Dr. Lu all love it when I buy a treat loaf of white bread,

but Bear is wholeheartedly a brown bread eater when it comes to his beloved turkey sandwiches.

This strata is lovely accompanied by a simple salad dressed in a lemon-garlic vinaigrette. Mom 2 always has a salad with dinner. One of my favorites of all time had a vinaigrette very like the one in this recipe. Tart with citrus, savory with Parmesan, and pungent with garlic, it creates the perfect foil for the rich strata.

This recipe is nicely savory with cheese, sausage, and mushrooms.

Strata

8 eggs

1 cup milk

½ cup sour cream

½ teaspoon salt

Butter or nonstick cooking spray

2 cups bread, cut in ½-inch cubes

8 large white or crimini mushrooms, sliced ¼-inch thick

1 cup grated/crumbled sharp cheese

1 cup cooked and crumbled bacon or sausage

Whisk the eggs, milk, sour cream, and salt together in a large bowl. Grease the inside of a large slow cooker. Layer the bread, mushrooms, cheese, and meat on the bottom of the slow cooker. Pour the egg mixture over all. Cook on low for 2–3 hours.

---

4 handfuls washed and torn lettuce

6 grape tomatoes, sliced

1 avocado, cut in ½-inch cubes

Add all ingredients to salad bowl.

½ cup extra-virgin olive oil

4 teaspoons lemon juice

2 tablespoons grated Parmesan

1 tablespoon mayonnaise

1 teaspoon sugar

½ teaspoon dried herb blend

½ teaspoon salt

1 clove garlic, pressed

Whisk ingredients together and season to taste. Toss thoroughly with the salad before serving.

 *Gluten-Free Variation:* Use **gluten-free bread**.

Tortilla Soup

Shortly before I began law school, I traveled to Central America in August to tour several Maya ruins. I'd taken a class in Maya archeology and culture and was fascinated with the history of this ancient civilization. The jungle was magical with lines of leaf-cutter ants, rasping calls of howler monkeys, and so many squawking, colorful birds. The crumbling ruins rose dramatically out of the jungle and were a haunting reminder of this ancient civilization. While visiting Tikal, Guatemala, my group had lunch on an outdoor terrace outside of the main plaza. There was no cooling beyond what the breeze provided, and so we sat and sweated as we waited for our lunch, which we were surprised to find was a hot soup.

In that moment, my whole perception of soup changed completely. It was remarkably satisfying and pleasant, despite the fact that I was as hot as I had ever been. It was almost as if I was becoming part of the heat as I sipped hot soup on a hot day. Soup has a place even in the heat, and it can be delicious there. Soup is a great option the year round.

In this tortilla soup the hearty, nutty flavor of the chickpeas complements the spicy salsa, tangy cheese, and salty chips. Homemade guacamole is the icing on the cake for this fantastic soup. However, if chickpeas are not your favorite, you could use five chicken thighs, cooked in 6 cups of chicken broth (about 3 cans), instead.

8 cups water

1½ cups dry chickpeas

2 teaspoon salt

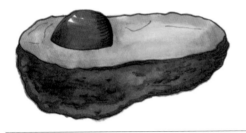

Soak the beans overnight, if possible. When ready to begin cooking, drain and rinse the beans.

Alternatively, bring the beans to a boil. Boil for 2 minutes, then add the salt. Turn off the heat and allow to soak for an hour. When ready to begin cooking, drain and rinse the beans.

You can also just cook the beans without soaking, but unsoaked beans may cause a bit more gas than soaked beans.

---

8 cups water

1 teaspoon oregano

1 medium dried chili (ribs and seeds removed for less heat)

½ teaspoon salt

Add beans and these ingredients to the slow cooker. Cook on high for 3–4 hours or on low for 6–8 hours. Test beans to see if they are tender. Taste stock and adjust seasonings.

1½ cups (or 2 rice cooker cups) jasmine rice

2 cloves garlic, pressed

Combine in rice cooker or pot. Cook according to package instructions

---

Guacamole

1 jalapeño pepper (ribs and seeds removed for less heat)

1 shallot

1 clove garlic, pressed

¼ teaspoon salt

2 large or 4 small avocados

2-3 tablespoons fresh lime juice

Chop the jalapeño pepper and the shallot finely. Toss the pepper, shallot, and garlic with salt. Allow mixture to sit for at least 10 minutes. Mash avocados into the pepper mixture. Stir in lime juice 1 tablespoon at a time and taste. Adjust the lime and salt to your personal taste. Try not to eat it all before dinner!

---

1 (16-ounce) container prepared salsa

1 cup crumbled cotija or feta cheese

1 cup frozen corn kernels, heated

½ bunch cilantro, chopped

1 lime, cut into 6 sections

Tortilla chips

Place the guacamole, salsa, cheese, corn, cilantro, lime sections, and tortilla chips in individual bowls and arrange on the table. Scoop rice into serving bowls and top with beans and broth. Serve with accompaniments for each person to personalize at the table.

 Gluten-Free Variation: This soup is naturally gluten-free. Make sure to use **gluten-free tortilla chips**.

Green and Gold Bean Stew

Several years ago, my family had an experience that has become etched—and romanticized—in our memories. Just before Thanksgiving, our city was blasted with a record-breaking windstorm. Near-hurricane-force winds pummeled ancient ponderosa pines, many of which fell, some onto power lines. As they fell, our lights flickered and went out, the furnace ground to a halt, and we were plunged into a cold darkness that lasted a week! Two people were killed, and thousands of us wondered whether we would get power in time for Thanksgiving! School was cancelled. People pulled out chain saws to cut apart the trees that littered the yards and streets. Electrical workers spent countless hours repairing the downed power lines. There was a great sense of banding together to help each other.

Thankfully, the building where my family attends church had not lost power. A group of us gathered there one evening to cook food that would otherwise have gone bad in our silent refrigerators and freezers. I'm not sure what I cooked that night beyond roasted cabbage. I cored the cabbage, cut it into strips, put the strips on a baking sheet—topping them with oil, dried herbs, and salt—then roasted them until the tips were brown and the cabbage velvety smooth. Every time I make this recipe it brings back memories of huddling together in our cold house and banding together with our community. It was a rough week, but, like the sharp cabbage that mellows in the oven's heat, the edges of "the windstorm" in my memory have been softened by time, distance, and a little grace.

5 cups water 1 pound navy beans 1½ teaspoons salt	Soak the beans overnight, if possible. When ready to begin cooking, drain and rinse the beans. Alternatively, bring the beans to a boil. Boil for 2 minutes, then add the salt. Turn off the heat and allow to soak for an hour. When ready to begin cooking, drain and rinse the beans. You can also just cook the beans without soaking, but unsoaked beans may cause a bit more gas than soaked beans.
6 cups water 1 teaspoon dried herb blend 1 teaspoon smoked paprika 2 cloves garlic, pressed	Rinse the beans and place them in the slow cooker. Add water, herbs, and garlic. Cover and cook on low for 6–8 hours or high for 3–4 hours.
½ teaspoon salt	Stir salt into the beans. Taste the beans and add additional salt as needed to enhance the flavor of the beans.
Gold rice 1½ cups (or 2 rice cooker cups) jasmine rice ½ teaspoon turmeric ½ teaspoon dried herb blend	After you begin the beans, add the rice to a rice cooker and add water as directed. Sprinkle the turmeric and herbs over the water and stir to combine. Cook. If you do not use a rice cooker, cook the rice on the stovetop according to package instructions adding the turmeric and herbs immediatly before serving the beans.
½ small green cabbage ¼ cup olive oil 1 teaspoon Italian herb seasoning blend ½ teaspoon salt	Preheat the oven to 425 degrees F. Core and slice cabbage crosswise into ½-inch-wide slices. If your children prefer raw vegetables, reserve a handful of sliced cabbage for them. Scatter remaining cabbage on a rimmed half-sheet pan. Drizzle oil over the top of the cabbage. Sprinkle with herbs and salt. Bake for 15 minutes and stir the cabbage. Bake an additional 10 minutes and remove from the oven when the cabbage is soft and the tips are toasty. **>**

Green and Gold Bean Stew

½ cup mayonnaise 1 garlic clove, pressed 1 lemon, juiced	Combine and place in a bowl to serve with the other accompaniments.
1 bunch parsley, chopped 1 (6-ounce) container brined feta cheese, crumbled Ridge-cut potato chips, crumbled	Arrange toppings in individual bowls on the table. Serve stew by placing some cabbage and ½ cup gold rice in a bowl. Ladle ½ cup of beans and ¼ cup of broth over the rice and cabbage. Diners can top their stew with their favorite toppings.

Gluten-Free Variation: This recipe is naturally gluten-free. Make sure that your **potato chips** are gluten-free.

Seven-Layer Dip
with Tortilla Chips and Crudités

When I was a little girl, I looked forward to my family's trips from our home near Seattle, Washington, to visit my maternal extended family in southeastern Idaho—in spite of the thirteen hours it took to drive there. That drive was my first real exercise in endurance. As the landscape became more arid and the houses further apart, I knew I was getting close to a place almost magical in its wildness and freedom. I knew I'd roam around town with my cousins and walk to the variety store with $1 bills from Grandma-Great to buy as much candy as possible. We would ride in the back of Grandpa's pickup out to visit the sheep or horses. And, of course, we'd eat family dinners with heaps of homestyle food like buttery homemade rolls, Idaho potatoes, juicy leg-o-lamb, tangy salads with peppers and iceberg

lettuce, pickled beets—and ice cream for dessert.

While regular dinners at Grandma's were definitely substantial, celebration dinners and Sunday dinners were hours-long events. We started with appetizers, worked our way into dinner, and eventually trickled into dessert. One popular appetizer was known as seven-layer dip. I loved it. There was something wonderful about the salty crunch of a tortilla chip against the smoothness of the sour cream and cheese, and the spicy sourness of the bright red salsa. Like a sort of southwestern fondue, seven-layer dip is wonderful with a variety of dippers. It's a hearty enough appetizer to stand in for dinner. Here seasoned meat is replaced with a rich vegetable layer to create a wholly vegetarian dinner. **>**

Seven-Layer Dip with Tortilla Chips and Crudités

Prep Time: 45 minutes · *Cook Time:* 4-8 hours · *Servings:* 4-6

4 cups water 1 cup dry pinto beans 2 teaspoons salt	Soak the beans overnight, if possible. When ready to begin cooking, drain and rinse the beans. Alternatively, bring the beans to a boil. Boil for 2 minutes, then add the salt. Turn off the heat and allow to soak for an hour. When ready to begin cooking, drain and rinse the beans. You can also just cook the beans without soaking, but unsoaked beans may cause a bit more gas than soaked beans.
1 large clove garlic, peeled and halved 1 dried chili 1 bay leaf 6 cups water	Rinse the soaked beans and place them in a slow cooker with the remaining ingredients. Cook on high for 3–4 hours or on low for 6–8 hours.
3 tablespoons oil 1 medium onion, cut in ¼-inch dice 1 red bell pepper, seeded and cut in ¼-inch dice 2 ribs celery, cut in ¼-inch dice 1 (14-ounce) can diced tomatoes, undrained 1 teaspoon salt 1 tablespoon cumin 1 teaspoon oregano 1 teaspoon smoked paprika 1 clove garlic, pressed	Heat the oil in a sauté pan over medium-high heat. Add the remaining ingredients and cook, stirring frequently, until the mixture comes to a simmer. Reduce the heat to medium-low and simmer for about 15 minutes. Stir the vegetables occasionally, until they are nicely melded together and soft.
¼ teaspoon salt	Sprinkle the cooked beans with salt. Use a potato masher or large whisk to break up the beans until they are mostly smooth. Taste and adjust salt. Spread the beans in the bottom of an 8x8-inch baking pan. Spread the onion mixture over the beans.

1 cup prepared guacamole	Spread over the onion mixture.
1½ cups sour cream ½ teaspoon chili powder 1 clove garlic, pressed ¼ teaspoon salt 1 lime, juiced ¼ cup cilantro leaves, chopped	Stir ingredients together until sauce is smooth, then spread over the guacamole.
1½ cups salsa	Spread evenly over the sour cream mixture.
2 cups grated cheddar or Mexican blend cheese	Sprinkle evenly over the salsa.
1 (3.8-ounce) can sliced black olives, drained 3 green onions, sliced	Sprinkle evenly over the cheese.
1 bag tortilla chips 2 carrots, peeled and cut into sticks 1 small jicama, peeled and cut into sticks 3 ribs celery, cut into sticks	Place the chips in bowls and arrange the vegetables on a plate. Serve with the dip.

Gluten-Free Variation: This recipe is **naturally gluten-free**. Make sure that your **chips** are also gluten-free.

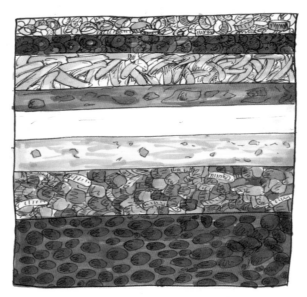

Asian Chicken Lettuce Wraps
with Crunchy Potato Chips

I love Asian foods. While I don't pretend to be an expert on any of them, one of my favorite things to do is wander around an Asian market and smell the unfamiliar scents that mingle in such a characteristic way. My daughter Nancy D loves to join me. I haven't decided if it's because she knows that I'll probably cave and buy her the little crème-filled panda cookies, or if she just delights in the colorful labels with their fascinating writing and whimsical artwork. Since she is my taste adventurer and is willing to try just about anything—with a special emphasis on savory foods—I suspect that it is a little of both.

These lettuce wraps are really savory in all of the good ways, but they are a little frustrating to eat. The lettuce tends to tear and let the filling spill out. A little patience and lots of napkins go a long way; the result is both delicious and fun. If it's not your style to have messy fingers, you could also serve this as a fun summer salad with a crusty bread instead of potato chips.

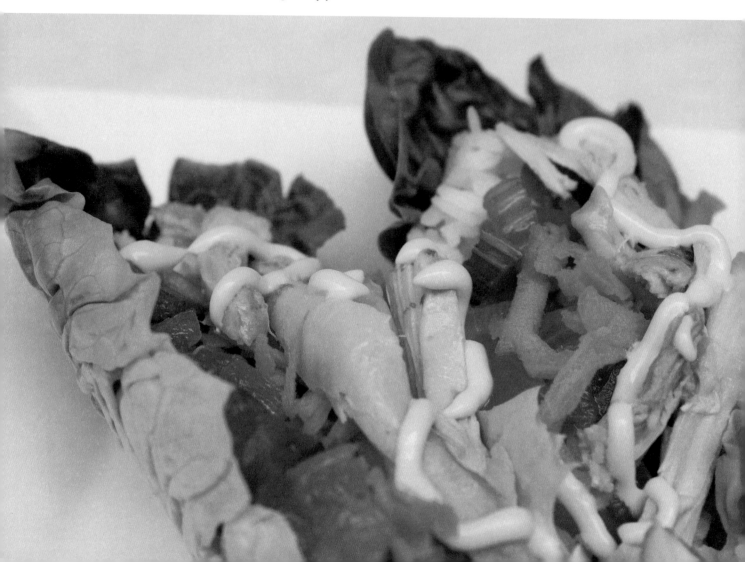

Butter or nonstick cooking spray

6 bone-in skin-on chicken thighs

4 cloves garlic, pressed

2 inches fresh ginger, peeled and grated

1 tablespoon brown sugar

2 tablespoons fish sauce

½ to 1 teaspoon chili paste

Grease the slow cooker. Add the chicken to the cooker. Combine the remaining ingredients and spread the sauce over the chicken. Cook on low for about 2½ to 3 hours. When the chicken reaches 160 degrees F, remove it from the slow cooker, place it on a plate, and tent it with foil. Reserve the cooking juices.

2¼ cups (or 3 rice cooker cups) Calrose rice

Cook according to package or rice cooker instructions. If using a rice cooker, start the rice at the same time as the chicken.

---

1 red bell pepper, seeded and cut in ¼-inch dice

3 cloves garlic, peeled and thinly sliced

1 small onion, cut in ¼-inch dice

2 ribs celery, cut in ¼-inch dice

Skim the fat off the top of the reserved cooking juices and add it to a large sauté pan over medium heat. Add the vegetables and cook, stirring constantly until the vegetables become translucent, about 5 minutes. Pour the reserved chicken juices over the vegetables, increase the heat to high, and simmer until the liquid thickens, and the vegetables are soft and lovely.

---

1 large carrot, peeled and grated

½ teaspoon rice vinegar

Pinch salt

Combine and set aside.

---

1 head Bibb or iceberg lettuce

Separate the lettuce leaves and rinse. Place them upside down on a clean towel to drain.

---

1 (13-ounce) bag kettle-cooked potato chips

Lime wedges

Sweet chili sauce

Mayonnaise

Sriracha sauce

Arrange rice, chicken, sautéed vegetables, carrots, lime wedges, chili sauce, mayonnaise, sriracha, and lettuce in small separate bowls on the table for diners to dress their wraps as desired. Serve chips on the side.

Gluten-Free Variation: Make sure you choose **gluten-free kettle-cooked potato chips**.

Sweet and Spicy Turkey Carnitas Taco Salad

Carnitas were in the first "real" taco that I ever ate and I was immediately taken by the contrast between the crispy tips and the meltingly rich interior of the meat. This meat was so far beyond the beef mixed with a packet of "taco seasoning" I was used to, I had difficulty seeing them as comparable. While this recipe won't produce authentic carnitas, it's much more approachable for a home cook. I use turkey drumsticks instead of pork because my digestive system is not a fan. If you and pork are in a happy place, you could sear a two-pound pork loin roast, then add it to the slow cooker instead of the drumsticks. Then shred the cooked meat and spread it on a rimmed half-sheet pan with the cooking juices. Broil for

3–5 minutes, or until the liquid thickens and the meat tips become toasty.

Although I like this meat in a taco with crumbled queso fresco and thinly sliced red onions, I really love it in a salad with a lovely dressing. In college, I was introduced to this kind of taco salad, where instead of a fried tortilla bowl, there was a fresh tortilla, and instead of dry salad and lackluster taco-bar toppings, there was a cilantro-lime vinaigrette. It was a wonderful melding of flavor and texture.

This salad takes some time to get together, but the flavors are fantastic, and it is definitely a satisfying dinner salad, especially for company, since it can be made almost entirely ahead of time.

1 (12-ounce) glass bottle imported cola	Pour cola into a saucepan and bring it to a boil. Boil for 10–12 minutes until it becomes thick and syrupy.
3–4 turkey drumsticks, skin on 1½ teaspoons dried oregano 1 tablespoon ground cumin 2 teaspoons smoked paprika 1 onion, cut in ¼-inch slices 6 cloves garlic, peeled and smashed ½ teaspoon lime zest 3 tablespoons lime juice ¼ cup brown sugar 1 teaspoon salt concentrated cola from first step	Place turkey drumsticks in the slow cooker. Add the remaining ingredients evenly over the top. Replace cover and cook on low for 7–8 hours or high for 4–5 hours or until the turkey is so tender it falls off the bone.
2¼ cups (or 3 rice cooker cups) jasmine rice 1 clove garlic, pressed ¼ cup cilantro, finely chopped	Combine rice and garlic in cooking pot or rice cooker. Add water as directed on package or in cooker instructions and cook. Stir in cilantro when rice is finished.
Vinaigrette ½ cup fresh lime or lemon juice ½ cup oil ½ cup mayonnaise 2 cloves garlic, pressed ¼ cup cilantro, finely chopped 2 tablespoons sugar 1 teaspoon salt	Whisk together vigorously to emulsify. Chill in the refrigerator.
6 cups lettuce or ½ medium cabbage	Wash and dry. Tear lettuce or chop cabbage. Keep cold.
1 cup cooked pinto beans	Rinse in colander and allow to drain. Warm beans. >

Sweet and Spicy Turkey Carnitas Taco Salad

Ingredients	Instructions
1 (10-ounce) package cotija cheese, crumbled 1 cup salsa 1 avocado, sliced ¼-inch thick 1 shallot, sliced thinly in rings	Place in individual serving bowls.
	Remove the turkey from the slow cooker and allow it to rest, covered, for 15 minutes. Remove skin and shred the turkey. While the turkey rests, strain the cooking juices to remove the onion and garlic. Bring the cooking juices to a boil over high heat and simmer until the liquid thickens so that a spatula dragged across the bottom of the pan leaves a track. Stir the sauce into the turkey.
12 uncooked tortillas	Cook according to package instructions.
	Place ingredients in serving bowls. Build your salad by placing a tortilla on a plate, followed by meat, beans, rice, greens, cheese, and salsa. Drizzle with vinaigrette and eat immediately.

Gluten-Free Variation: Make corn tortillas by combining 2 cups/240 grams **masa harina corn flour**, ¼ teaspoon **salt**, and 1½ cups **water** in a mixing bowl. Combine until the dough feels like fresh playdough. Preheat a griddle to medium heat (350 degrees F). Make golf ball–sized balls and roll between parchment or heavy-duty plastic bags (or press in a tortilla press) to about ⅛-inch thick. Place on the griddle and cook for 30 seconds. Flip tortilla and press down the edges with a spatula. Continue to cook for an additional minute and a half. If you're lucky, the tortilla will puff a bit. Remove the tortilla to a plate and cover it with a cloth to keep warm and continue pressing and cooking the rest of the tortillas. If you do not need all the tortillas for dinner, save some of the dough to make **elephant ears** by preheating about ½-inch **oil** in the bottom of a 10-inch sauté pan over medium heat. When hot, press then fry the remaining tortillas in the hot oil, about 1 minute per side. Drain on paper towels and sprinkle with cinnamon sugar. Eat immediately. These are so yummy!

How to Shop

Grocery shopping is stressful for some people and relaxing for others. While some of this depends entirely on the individual and his or her interest in food, it may also be attributed to making smart choices about when, where, and how to shop. The following recommendations may help brighten your grocery shopping experience regardless of your current sentiment toward shopping.

Thoroughly plan your menus before you go shopping. Have an idea of how much you'll spend and what you need to purchase.

Arrange your grocery list to match the layout of the store. For instance, if you always begin with produce, list all produce items first. This helps avoid wasting time backtracking or returning to the store for items you missed.

Think about how often you need to shop and how that can fit into your schedule. While once-weekly shopping allows for fresher produce, it may not work well if you have to travel a long distance to reach the store. When planning menus, consider using perishable ingredients earlier, and nonperishable ingredients later. Unless you're a college student with only a mini fridge in your dorm room (or something similar), it's probably best to avoid shopping on a daily basis; doing so can add unnecessary stress to your schedule and is likely to add unnecessary expense to your budget.

Be social while you're shopping. Smile at or chat with other shoppers and the grocery workers—especially if you're feeling impatient, bored, or frustrated with the process.

When shopping with small children, offer a small reward for good behavior, such as a free sample from the bakery. This can be very effective, particularly if you don't allow the treat when the child really does behave badly.

Swedish Meatballs
with Roasted Potatoes and Green Peas

If there is one dinner that defines Dad's side of our family, this is it. Swedish meatballs traditionally anchor our family's formal Christmas Eve dinner. They, along with mashed potatoes and gravy, rolls, Jell-O salad, and chocolate angel food cake (see p. 140), make up the stuff of legend in our family. There is always a contest to see who can make the best number of meatballs that are uniformly about ¾-inch in diameter and rolled tightly enough to avoid disintegration in the cooking process. When she first began hosting Christmas dinner, Mimi would roll and cook over 300 meatballs by herself! One year she decided she had had enough and asked Papa and her sons to help roll the meatballs. Eventually this

became a family tradition anticipated just as much as the family Christmas pageant that followed the dinner. The number of meatballs made is carefully tallied each year; Papa, Dad, and my Uncle John were always sticklers about making consistently sized meatballs. The number of meatballs made never matches the number served, however. Sneaky fingers, both big and small, find their way into the roasting pan all day long.

Swedish meatballs are a great entree for holidays and company dinners because they can be finished entirely ahead of time. The batch can be doubled, but you will need to use two slow cookers or a covered pot in the oven to contain them all.

1 pound ground beef	Preheat the broiler to high. Add the ingredients to a large bowl. Mash and fold together with fingertips until the mixture is homogeneous. Gently roll into ¾- to 1-inch balls and place on a rimmed half-sheet pan. Broil 3 minutes. Add meatballs to slow cooker and cook on low for 2–3 hours.
1 pound ground veal (if unavailable, use beef)	
1 pound ground pork	
½ cup boxed potato flakes	
1 shallot, minced	
3 cloves garlic, pressed	
1 egg	
2 teaspoons salt	
½ teaspoon pepper	
1 pint heavy cream	Pour the cream into a saucepan over medium heat. Add the mushrooms and salt and bring to a simmer over high heat. Reduce the temperature to medium-low and simmer until the cream thickens and the mushrooms soften, approximately 15 minutes.
8 ounces crimini mushrooms, chopped	
½ teaspoon salt	
8 medium Yukon Gold potatoes	Preheat the oven to 425 degrees F. Cut the potatoes into ½-inch chunks. Toss with olive oil and spread on a rimmed half-sheet pan. Sprinkle with salt and herbs and roast for 20 minutes. Carefully slide a spatula under the potatoes, turn, and cook an additional 5–10 minutes until tender and crisp.
⅓ cup olive oil	
½ teaspoon salt	
½ teaspoon dried herb blend	
1 (16-ounce) package frozen petite green peas	Place peas in a pot and just cover with water. Place over high heat and just bring to boil. Remove from heat immediately and serve with the meatballs, mushroom sauce, and potatoes.

Gluten-Free Variation: This dinner is naturally gluten-free.

The library is one of my favorite places. Checking out books is like going shopping with a budget that's only limited by how much I can carry. I remember discovering that libraries had cookbook sections in college. I didn't really have the time then, but after my children began arriving, the cookbook section was one of my favorite places to browse. Happily for me, our library was within walking distance for my kiddos, and so when we all needed a little break from being together at home, one of my favorite escapes was to the library. My kids enjoyed the children's books and toys, and I checked out as many cookbooks as I could. It was an almost effortless outing that perfectly met our needs—or at least until the baby decided that she was done and needed lunch.

Several years ago in my cookbook browsing, I found a book about cooking a month's worth of dinners in a day. I was immediately interested. Cooking once and then being done with it, particularly the daily washing up, sounded like a great idea to me. For one reason or another, however, I never did manage to make that work in my own kitchen. But I do like to have meals in the freezer I can use when prep time gets swallowed up by a school project, a delightful conversation with a friend, or a lovely day outside. Doubling these recipes can give you a dinner tonight and a dinner for later. Your future self will thank you when the inevitable wrench gets thrown in the works.

Frozen Dinners

WHEN YOU GIVE YOURSELF A PRESENT
30 to 60 Minutes Prep

English Muffin Mini Pizzas

with Green Salad

Mr. Kent rides the bus. And the train. And motorized scooters. And walks. He prefers to get around without a car whenever possible. He may have asked me out on a second date in part because I was willing to ride the bus and trolley—and do a lot of walking—on our first afternoon together. His penchant for being multimodal makes it possible for us to have only one car. As a practical matter, that reduces our expenses as well as our impact on the earth. Not only does this keep Mr. Kent happy, it also allows me a little extra money to support my organic vegetable and animal product preferences. It's a win-win, and we all feel healthier because of it.

However, that doesn't mean having one car is simple. It's definitely not. But Mr. Kent also revels in complex transit plans. It's not uncommon for me to pack up the kiddos to visit relatives a few days earlier than Mr. Kent so he can join us by plane, bus—or sometimes train! I like to leave dinners in the freezer for him so that he can avoid grazing. Not that he can't cook, but cooking a meal for one—even heating something up—is harder when you're just home from work and hungry. Unless you're really prepared, it rarely ends without a lot of snacking, and then what's the point of eating what you've made, especially if you're eating alone? These make-ahead English muffin mini pizzas are a great option—they're simple to make and quick to reheat. These also make a great lunch or after-school snack.

6 English muffins 2 cloves garlic 1 cup marinara sauce	Preheat the oven broiler and place the rack 6 inches from the broiler. Split the muffins and place them on a half-sheet pan. Broil briefly while watching, until the tops are just crusty but not brown. Scrape the tops with the garlic. Allow the muffins to cool. Spread each muffin with about a tablespoon of marinara sauce.
Toppings ½ cup meats (pepperoni, cooked sausage, bacon bits) ¼ cup fruits (tomatoes, pineapple chunks, olives) ¼ cup caramelized onions ¼ cup pesto 2 cups shredded mozzarella ¼ cup grated Parmesan cheese Garlic salt	Add desired toppings to the pizzas. Kids like to decorate their own pizzas. Sprinkle each pizza with a bit of garlic salt. Freeze the pizzas on the baking sheet, then transfer them to a freezer container or bag after they're frozen.
¼ cup olive oil	To cook, preheat the oven to 400 degrees F. Drizzle each pizza with a teaspoon of olive oil. Bake the pizzas for 7–10 minutes, or until they're hot and the cheese is toasty. >

Salad

1 head romaine lettuce

½ cup grated Parmesan cheese

½ cup crunchy croutons

Salad dressing

⅓ cup olive oil

1 tablespoon white wine vinegar

2 tablespoons honey

1 teaspoon prepared mustard

2 teaspoons water

¼ teaspoon salt

1 clove garlic, pressed

½ teaspoon Italian herb seasoning blend

1 pinch red pepper flakes

Gluten-Free Variation: Use **gluten-free English muffins**. Be sure to toast them thoroughly in the first step.

Wash and dry the lettuce and add to salad bowl with cheese and croutons. Use your favorite bottled dressing, or whisk dressing ingredients together. Toss with salad immediately before serving.

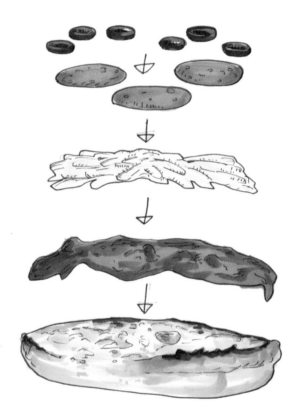

Chicken and Corn Casserole
with Sautéed Cabbage

Casseroles with ground meat, cheese, and a crunchy topping are ubiquitous both as comfort food and as pillars of 1950s Americana. I can see the magazine and cookbook photographs of nicely coiffed, aproned women smiling widely over the casseroles they're presenting to their adoring families. These women never looked harried or overburdened by their dinner preparations. While this may be partially attributed to the inevitable cream of chicken/celery/mushroom soup that made up most of the casserole, it is largely because casseroles are easy dinners that produce minimal mess. Their children also seemed to always be excited about casseroles—even with mushrooms and cooked celery. Honestly, it's hit-and-miss with my kids and casseroles, but they like this one.

While I don't usually don heels and pearls to accompany my nice dress and frilled apron before I sally forth into the kitchen to prepare dinner, these accoutrements would not be any worse for the wear if I should choose to glam it up a bit when I make this casserole. It's easy, it registers pretty low on the mess scale, and it's really tasty. This recipe makes two casseroles—one for now, one for later. What more could a cook ask for—at least on a busy night? >

Chicken and Corn Casserole with Sautéed Cabbage

Prep Time: 30 minutes · *Cook Time:* 1 hour · *Servings:* 4-6

Ingredients	Instructions
2 tablespoons olive oil 2 onions, diced 1½ teaspoons salt 4 cloves garlic, pressed 2 pounds ground chicken 2 tablespoons cumin 2 teaspoons smoked paprika 2 teaspoons oregano	Heat the oil in a large sauté pan over medium-high heat. Add the onion and salt and cook, stirring frequently, until the onion turns golden and soft. Add the garlic and cook for 30 seconds before adding the chicken and spices. Break up the chicken and brown, stirring frequently, approximately 3–5 minutes.
1 (12-ounce) can tomato paste ⅓ cup masa harina 2½ cups water ¼ to 1 teaspoon chili powder (to taste) 1 teaspoon salt 1 teaspoon garlic powder 1 teaspoon onion powder	Whisk together to combine.
Butter or nonstick cooking spray 2 cups shredded sharp cheddar cheese 2 cups frozen corn	Lightly grease two 8-inch square baking dishes. Spread half of the chicken over the bottom of each dish and repeat with the cheese and corn. Pour the tomato sauce evenly over chicken, cheese, and corn. Cover and freeze the casseroles at this point if you are not using immediately.
4 cups corn chips (per casserole)	Preheat the oven to 375 degrees F. Crush chips lightly and sprinkle over the chicken mixture. Bake uncovered for 25–30 minutes unfrozen or 1 hour frozen, adding the corn chips halfway through.

½ medium-sized head green cabbage

3 tablespoons olive oil

½ teaspoon salt

Slice the cabbage into strips about ¼-inch thick. If your children prefer raw vegetables, reserve a handful of sliced cabbage for them. Heat the oil in a sauté pan over medium-high heat. Add the sliced cabbage and sprinkle with salt. Cook, stirring frequently, until the cabbage edges begin to brown and it becomes soft. Check seasonings and add additional salt to taste. Serve casserole with additional cabbage and corn chips.

Gluten-Free Variation: Check to make sure that your **chips** are gluten-free.

Party Appetizers for No Particular Reason

When I was growing up, and, really, as an adult before my celiac diagnosis, I loved going to any kind of party where appetizers would be expected. The texture and flavor palates ranged from crunchy to soft and savory to sweet and sour. I often liked the appetizers so much that it was difficult for me to restrain myself and save some space for the main event. With this dinner, there is no need to try to do that because the appetizers *are* dinner. Collect some of your favorite noshes from your favorite frozen food section (if you happen to have a Trader Joe's nearby, they have the best and most fun options), stow them in the freezer, and you can have a fun dinner without much preparation. Nancy D likes to help me pick out fun appetizers. Her favorites are mini sausages wrapped in puff pastry and pork-stuffed soft Chinese buns called bao.

1 baguette 1 clove garlic, halved 1 (8-ounce) jar bruschetta topping	Wrap the baguette to freeze or buy a fresh one on the day you need it. You will thaw it at room temperature. Cut ½-inch-thick angled slices of bread. Toast the bread until it is golden and rub the cut side of the garlic clove lightly on the bread. Allow the toast to cool slightly. Top with a spoonful of purchased bruschetta topping and arrange on a plate to serve.
1 (10.5-ounce) package frozen pigs in a blanket (such as Trader Joe's Pastry Pups)	Heat and brown according to package instructions.
1 (22-ounce) package frozen orange chicken 1 tablespoon toasted sesame seeds Toothpicks	Bake chicken according to package instructions. Heat the accompanying sauce and toss the chicken in the sauce. Skewer with toothpicks and sprinkle with toasted sesame seeds.
1 (13-ounce) package frozen large soft pretzels Mustard	Bake the pretzels according to package instructions. Allow to cool slightly and cut the pretzels into bite-sized portions. Serve with mustard.
1 (10-ounce) container prepared artichoke dip 2 large carrots, peeled 1 red bell pepper 1 rib celery	Because it is good to have a few vegetables, heat up the artichoke dip according to package instructions. Cut the vegetables into sticks and arrange on a plate with the artichoke dip in a dish.

Gluten-Free Variation: Sadly, this menu does not translate well to serve gluten-free eaters.

FROZEN DINNERS

63

Meatloaf
with Roasted Broccoli and Mashed Potatoes

The dinner table can become a battleground. I'm not sure how many times I've had a conversation with my children about subjective opinions and objective realities, but it's certainly a difficult lesson to learn. They continue to argue to the death (of any conversation, at least) about whether soup is good or mushrooms are gross. It's hard for them to make space for another's differing opinion about food. While it can be obnoxious—and frankly frustrating—to have these battles, we keep having them, and we keep working on it. How can I expect public debate to improve if I fail to teach the basics of it in my own home? So I allow the inane arguments to begin, and I keep reminding my kiddos to reconsider whether they're arguing

productively, or whether they're just arguing for the sake of arguing. We're working on it.

Meatloaf and mashed potatoes is one of those divisive dinners at our table. While Mr. Kent and Nancy D are huge fans, Hervor *really* dislikes meatloaf. *All* meatloaf. Even *this* meatloaf. I can't blame her—while it tastes really good, meatloaf is pretty homely in both name and appearance. Sometimes I wish I could just blindfold my kiddos before they eat. Then the meatloaf might just pass as a beloved open-faced burger! Despite its lack of allure, I hope that you will give meatloaf a chance. This classic diner fare feels very homey, especially when accompanied with mashed potatoes and gravy and roasted broccoli. Leftover meatloaf is an excellent addition to marinara sauce.

1 tablespoon oil 1 onion, finely chopped ½ teaspoon salt 2 cloves garlic, pressed	Add the oil to a large sauté pan over medium heat. Add onions and salt and sauté, stirring frequently, until translucent, approximately 5–6 minutes. Add the garlic and cook, stirring constantly, for about 30 seconds more. Remove from the heat and set aside.
1 (1-pound) package fresh ground turkey 1 (1-pound) package fresh ground turkey sausage 2 eggs 2 tablespoons fish sauce ½ cup potato flakes ½ cup ketchup	Place the meat in a large bowl and break up into big chunks. Thoroughly combine all ingredients by cutting them together with a spatula or your fingers. Spread the mixture about ½ inch thick in a freezer container or bag and freeze.
3 pounds Yukon Gold potatoes, quartered 6 medium cloves garlic, peeled ½ cup butter, softened ¼ cup cream 1 teaspoon salt	Add potatoes and garlic to a large pot and cover with water. Bring to a boil and cook until they are quite soft, approximately 15–20 minutes. Run potatoes and garlic through a potato ricer into a large bowl. Stir in the butter, cream, and salt. Check seasonings and cool completely. Spoon into a resealable container and freeze.
	Thaw the meatloaf mix and potatoes overnight in the refrigerator. Preheat the oven to 375 degrees F. Adjust the racks so the broccoli pan will fit under the meatloaf pan. Press the meat mixture into a loaf pan and bake approximately 1 hour, until the internal temperature is 160 degrees F. >

Meatloaf with Roasted Broccoli and Mashed Potatoes

Gravy

4 cups good chicken or turkey stock

1 tablespoon beef bouillon paste

3 tablespoons cornstarch

1 tablespoon butter

Salt

Place 3 cups chicken broth and the bouillon paste in a sauté pan. Bring to simmer over high heat and reduce to maintain the simmer. Whisk together the remaining cup of cold broth and cornstarch in a small bowl. Whisk cornstarch mixture into the simmering broth and continue to whisk constantly until the gravy thickens. Remove from heat and stir in butter until it melts. Adjust the salt and keep warm.

---

2 large heads broccoli, cut in florets

2 tablespoons olive oil

½ teaspoon salt

Cut up the broccoli into bite-sized pieces. Spread onto a rimmed half-sheet pan, drizzle with oil, and sprinkle with salt. Bake with the meatloaf for its last 20 minutes.

Reheat the potatoes by placing them in a microwave-safe dish, covering them with waxed paper, and microwaving for three minutes. Stir and test the temperature. Re-cover and cook for an additional three minutes as necessary.

Gluten-Free Variation: This recipe is naturally gluten-free.

Navy Bean Chili

with Cheesy Gorditas and Honey Butter

As a first grader, I was excited when my parents announced that we were going to begin skiing on Friday nights. It sounded like fun. It *was* fun to go shopping for the "car lunch" that we ate on our way to the mountain. It was also fun to chomp my way through puffed cheeseballs and store-bought cookies. I began to have some apprehension, however, as the road rose into the mountains, and I saw steep swaths where avalanches had been cleared from the roadway. I became sure that I was doomed to crash and die. By the time we reached the softly lit ski area with its creaking lifts and swooshing patrons, I was terrified. Despite the fact that I couldn't even see the road anymore, my little mind was still sure I would fall off the mountain.

It took years of superhuman patience on Dad's part, encouragement and lessons from both of my parents, and a lot of personal growth before I came to enjoy the sport of downhill skiing. During this long transition phase, my favorite part of any trip was always when we took a break for lunch. Chili was a perennial offering at the lodge lunch counters, and I loved how the deeply warming bites were gooey with melted cheese and salty with a crushed saltine.

Unlike those chilis, this chili is made with navy beans, plenty of chili flavor, and potatoes. Served with gorditas—a puffy corn masa cake—this chili is a great end to a chilly winter day. >

Navy Bean Chili with Cheesy Gorditas and Honey Butter

Prep Time: 1 hour · *Cook Time:* 2 hours · *Servings:* 6–8

8 cups water 1 pound/2 cups dried navy beans 1½ teaspoon salt	Soak the beans overnight, if possible. When ready to begin cooking, drain and rinse the beans. Alternatively, bring the beans to a boil. Boil for 2 minutes, then add the salt. Turn off the heat and allow to soak for an hour. When ready to begin cooking, drain and rinse the beans. You can also just cook the beans without soaking, but unsoaked beans may cause a bit more gas than soaked beans.
2 tablespoons olive oil 1 medium onion, cut in ¼-inch dice 1 red bell pepper, seeded and cut in ¼-inch dice 3 ribs celery, cut in ¼-inch dice 2–3 dried ancho chilis (ribs and seeds removed for less heat), torn into pieces 1 teaspoon salt 1 cup water	Add all ingredients except the water into a large Dutch oven over medium-high heat. Stir to coat. Cook, stirring frequently, until the onion is golden and all vegetables soften, approximately 15 minutes. Cool slightly, then add the water and puree the vegetable mixture until it is smooth.
7 cups water 3 cloves garlic, peeled and smashed 1 bay leaf 1 tablespoon smoked paprika	Drain and rinse the beans and add them to the Dutch oven with the ingredients listed here. Stir the chili puree into the beans. Bring to a simmer, cover, and cook until beans are meltingly tender, about 1 hour.
4 medium Yukon Gold potatoes, peeled	Cut the potatoes into ½-inch cubes and add to the bean pot. If you plan to serve the beans immediately, cook an additional 25–30 minutes or until the potatoes are meltingly tender. If you plan to freeze the chili, cook for about 10 minutes until the potatoes are more crisp-tender.

Salt	Discard the bay leaf. Taste the beans and add additional salt if they need it. Cool completely prior to freezing. Thaw in a covered pot over medium-low heat and make sure to stir it frequently to prevent burning.
Gorditas 3 cups/360 grams masa harina 2 teaspoons baking powder 1 teaspoon salt 3 tablespoons sugar ⅓ cup oil 2 cups water 1½ cups shredded sharp cheddar cheese	Preheat a griddle to medium-low (300 degrees F) heat. Combine all ingredients thoroughly into a mixture that resembles playdough. Form into 1½-inch balls and flatten to discs ½ inch thick. Cook approximately 5 minutes on each side. Remove to a plate and cover to keep warm.
½ cup butter, softened ¼ cup honey	Beat together until smooth and serve with gorditas.
1 cup crema 1 cup guacamole 1 handful cilantro, leaves and stems chopped 1 lime	Place chili in bowls. Drizzle tops with crema and sprinkle with cilantro. Serve with guacamole and a wedge of lime.

 **Gluten-Free Variation:** This recipe is naturally gluten-free.

In my opinion, dinners that require more preparation time than about one cumulative hour are labors of love. I started my experience with such dinners when I decided as a college sophomore to cater Kleine's high school graduation party. Incredibly, Mom agreed to let me do it! I'm still not sure whether she was really confident that I could pull it off, or whether I had just worn her down by whining about it (as a present-day mother I understand the power that whining can have, particularly when the person you're asking is already stressed). Whatever the reason, my mom agreed to let me play caterer. She helped me and pushed me to plan, and she definitely helped with preparations. There were a few moments of stress, but, ultimately, the party buffet was a success.

Many years later, I prepared my first major dinner without my mom's help when I hosted Thanksgiving for thirteen people. I was very pregnant with Nancy D, and I prepared days ahead. I made lists and timetables. I even made my own rough puff pastry for the wrapped mini sausages that we had as an appetizer. We had a memorable evening together at the makeshift long table in our living room, and it all felt very festive. Despite the fact that the apple pie was underdone because I had gambled on an experiment and lost, the evening was mostly a success. I was very thankful!

Timing is critical with these labors of love. There are usually many balls in the air at once, and it can be easy to lose your place. These are not dinners to attempt on weeknights unless you're home during the day with nothing else to do. (Riiiight!) These recipes are good occasional treats where the (hopefully fun) preparation should be an event in and of itself.

Time-Consuming Dinners

LABORS OF LOVE AND FLIGHTS OF FANCY
2 Hours to All Day

Classic Salad Bar
with Chickpea Socca

I remember going to a local Italian American restaurant with Mom and Dad, a classic restaurant of the 1960s and '70s with a whiff of stale cigarette smoke and garlic in the air. This restaurant fascinated me because its salad bar spanned an entire wall. I loved getting a little plate for the salad bar, which always seemed too small! There was iceberg lettuce with shredded carrots and red cabbage and rows of plastic canisters set in ice, full of mushrooms, peppers, various cheeses, tomatoes, cucumbers, carrots, pickled beets, olives, croutons, sunflower seeds, fruit gelatin, and about eight different dressings. It was so fun to build my little salad. I tried things there I might not have

been as excited about trying anywhere else.

Now that I'm grown and cooking for myself, I enjoy having a salad bar dinner on occasion. It's a fun way to introduce my children to new foods *and* encourage them to eat their vegetables. They like having a choice about which vegetables they're eating, and they tend to try new things when everything looks appealing. While this salad bar is not going to take up an entire wall, there are options for everyone. The accompanying flatbread, socca, is a griddle cake from the Provençal region of France. It's really yummy when fresh and warm, so don't be put off by the beany smell of the batter—this cooks away.

Socca

2 cups/240 grams chickpea flour

1¼ teaspoon salt

2 cups warm water

⅓ cup olive oil

Whisk together the flour and salt. Pour in the water and olive oil and whisk everything together until it is very smooth. The batter will be runny. Cover and set it aside for at least 30 minutes, preferably an hour or two.

---

3 eggs

Place a steamer basket in a saucepan and put an inch of water in the bottom. Set over high heat. Add eggs to the basket and cover. Once steam comes out from under the lid, turn the heat down to medium-low. Simmer for 10 minutes. Place the eggs in a bowl of ice water. Cool completely, peel, and chop. Place chopped eggs in a bowl.

---

2 ounces bacon

Cut the raw bacon into ½-inch pieces. Place in a cold frying pan over medium heat. Cook, stirring frequently, until the bacon is crispy. Drain on a paper towel. Place in a small bowl.

---

1 (¼-inch-thick) slice of deli roasted turkey or ham

Cut into ¼-inch cubes. Place in a bowl.

---

4 ounces cheese

Grate the cheese and place in a bowl.

---

1 cup sliced pickled beets

Drain and place in a dish.

---

1 cup chopped smoked and salted almonds

Place almonds in a bowl.

Garlicky Ranch Dressing

½ cup yogurt

½ cup mayonnaise

1 small lemon, juiced

1 small clove garlic, pressed

2 teaspoons sugar

¼ teaspoon salt

1 teaspoon dried dill

Whisk all ingredients together and add to a little pitcher or bowl. >

Classic Salad Bar with Chickpea Socca

1 heart romaine lettuce 1 pint cherry tomatoes 1 avocado	Wash and dry the lettuce. Tear leaves into pieces. Cut the tomatoes in half. Cut the avocado into ½-inch pieces. Place the tomatoes and avocado into separate bowls.
1 cup grated Parmesan cheese	Stir into the socca batter. Preheat a nonstick griddle or frying pan to 350 degrees F (medium heat). Pour ¼-cup dollops of batter on the preheated griddle. Cook until the top sets, about 5 minutes. Flip and cook an additional 2 minutes. Place cakes on a plate and cover to keep warm.
	Place a mound of lettuce on each diner's plate. Arrange all of the salad bar ingredients on the table and invite each person to make his or her own salad. Serve with warm socca.

(※) **Gluten-Free Variation:** This recipe is naturally gluten-free.

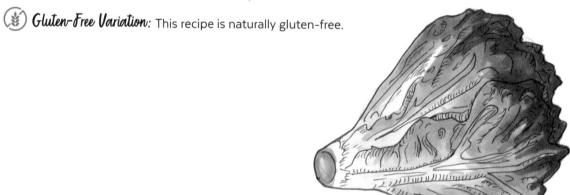

Sushi Rolls

I never thought to make sushi until my celiac diagnosis. Sushi-making should be reserved for professionals—or so I thought. However, restaurant sushi—particularly the yummy designer rolls—is a great hideout for wheat, so I had to decide between learning how to make it or never eating it again. I went with the former, and I'm glad I did! While I'm nowhere near a true sushi chef, I have learned some basic techniques and become familiar with ingredients that make it possible for me to enjoy sushi again. Yay! My kids all enjoy sushi night. Hervor loves classic California rolls, Bear prefers smoked salmon, Nancy D was delighted when I first made little pandas with nori and sushi rice. Dr. Lu is still just adjusting to sitting at the table, but she seems to enjoy sushi night.

Sushi can be a great place to use leftover fish, meats, cheese, and vegetables. Take a quick glance at your refrigerator before you go shopping and you may find your next favorite roll just waiting for you! Be creative and use complementary textures, such as toasted sesame seeds with smooth cream cheese, and you're on your way to a great new roll.

Before you try this recipe you will need to visit an Asian market to find a bamboo sushi rolling mat, nori, furikake seasoning, Japanese mayonnaise, and kombu. It would also be a really good idea to watch a couple of sushi rolling videos online (Kikkoman sponsors a few on YouTube) so you can get the idea. >

Sushi Rolls

3 cups (or 4 rice cooker cups) sushi rice

1 (1" x 3") piece kombu

⅓ cup rice vinegar

¼ cup sugar

1½ teaspoons salt

Cover the rice with water. Agitate it with your fingers until the water becomes cloudy. Carefully pour the water off to drain the rice. Repeat at least three times or until the water you pour off is clear. Fill the rice cooker with rice and water according to the manufacturer's instructions, add kombu, and cook. If you do not have a rice cooker, place washed rice and kombu into a pot with 6½ cups water. Bring to a simmer over high heat. Reduce heat to low and cover the pot. Cook for 20–25 minutes until the water is absorbed into the rice.

When rice has cooked, combine vinegar, sugar, and salt in a saucepan. Bring to a simmer and stir until the sugar and salt are dissolved. Remove kombu and discard. Put the rice in a large, shallow bowl. Pour vinegar mixture over rice and cut through the rice with a rice paddle or wooden spoon. Turn the sections of rice over and fan them to help cool the rice. Repeat until the rice is room temperature and the vinegar is totally absorbed. This may seem tedious, but it is very important to prevent the nori from splitting or growing soggy. Cover rice with a damp cloth.

Sharpen your best knife.

Sweet teriyaki sauce

⅓ cup soy sauce

¼ cup sugar

1 tablespoon rice vinegar

¼ teaspoon cornstarch

Combine in a saucepan—you can use the same pan you used for the sushi vinegar—and bring to a simmer over medium-high heat. Simmer for 1–2 minutes or until the sauce thickens. Set aside.

2 ounces cream cheese

1 ounce Colby-Jack cheese

Cut into ¼-inch-square strips.

Ingredients	Instructions
4–6 ounces cold smoked salmon	Cut salmon into ½-inch-wide strips no more than 10 inches long.
4 ounces imitation or fresh crab, separated 3 tablespoons Japanese mayonnaise ½ teaspoon sriracha	Finely chop or flake half of the crab and toss with the mayonnaise and sriracha.
1 cucumber	Cut into ¼-inch-square strips.
1 avocado	Cut into ¼ x ½-inch-wide strips.
4 teaspoons wasabi powder 3 teaspoons ice water	Combine thoroughly and allow to stand, covered, for about 5 minutes.
1 (5-ounce) package roasted nori sheets Bamboo sushi rolling mat Bowl of warm salt water Reserved teriyaki sauce Japanese mayonnaise Furikake	Place a sheet of nori on the bamboo mat with the shiny side against the bamboo. Scoop approximately one cup of rice onto the nori. Dip your fingers in the salt water and spread rice evenly over nori with your fingertips, leaving a 1-inch margin uncovered at the top. Be sure to spread to all other edges. Smear a small amount of wasabi on the edge closest you. Place desired filling(s) on top, near the middle of the rice. Make sure the edge of the nori sheet closest to you meets the edge of the bamboo mat. Roll bamboo mat until the edge meets the rice in the middle of the roll. Grasp the rolled portion with your whole hand. Gently but firmly squeeze all along the rolled portion while pulling the top edge of the mat along the table. Shift the bamboo mat so the top edge rolls over the rest of the roll. Repeat as needed to finish the roll. Cut the roll into ½-inch-thick slices, wiping your knife clean after each cut.

Good roll combinations

Crab salad, avocado, and furikake sprinkle

Smoked salmon and cream cheese

Smoked salmon, cucumber, and Japanese mayonnaise

Imitation crab, avocado, and sweet teriyaki sauce

Colby-Jack cheese and cucumber

Ingredients	Instructions
4 cups water 4 tablespoons miso paste 1 green onion, sliced thinly	Bring the water to a simmer. Remove from the heat. Whisk in the miso paste until it is suspended in the water. Garnish with green onion and serve in small cups.

Gluten-Free Variation: Make sure that you use **gluten-free soy sauce**, **gluten-free imitation crab**, and **gluten-free furikake**.

Brazilian Dinner

I had never thought much about Brazil prior to marrying Mr. Kent. I had been to a churrasco once or twice, and there I loved the cheese rolls, but I had never really tried to re-create any of the flavors. When we met during my final year of law school, and I learned that Mr. Kent had spent two years in Brazil as a missionary, I felt a renewed interest in Brazilian cooking. He introduced me to this riff on the classic Brazilian bean and pork stew, feijoada, which is not authentic because it does not contain 20 different pork parts, but it is delicious. He calls it feijoada Americana! This works well for us because we don't have a pig at our disposal—or 100 people to feed.

I love this stew with the accompaniments of marinated vegetables, roasted pineapple, and pão de queijo, which is well worth the extra effort of remembering to pick up tapioca starch. It might even be worth a special trip to the market if you forget the first time!

Mr. Kent looks forward to taking the rest of us to his beloved Brazil in a few years. I must say that the prospect of tropical jungle and sugar-sand beach is tremendously tempting. I don't think I will put up a fuss at all when he decides our budget can support the trip! When I get there, I will certainly try authentic feijoada, but for now, this will have to do.

4 cups water

1 cup black beans

1 teaspoon salt

Soak the beans overnight, if possible. When ready to begin cooking, drain and rinse the beans.

Alternatively, bring the beans to a boil. Boil for 2 minutes, then add the salt. Turn off the heat and allow to soak for an hour. When ready to begin cooking, drain and rinse the beans.

You can also just cook the beans without soaking, but unsoaked beans may cause a bit more gas than soaked beans.

---

5 cups water

1 bay leaf

⅛ teaspoon chili flakes

Rinse the black beans well in a colander and add them to a Dutch oven. Add the water, bay leaf, and chili flakes. Simmer uncovered for 1 hour or until the beans are very tender. Monitor the beans to make sure the water does not boil off.

Marinated zucchini

2 tablespoons lime juice

3 tablespoons oil

3 cloves garlic, pressed

½ teaspoon ground coriander

1 teaspoon salt

½ teaspoon smoked paprika

2 (10-inch) zucchini, sliced ½ inch thick

1 jalapeño pepper, cut in small dice
(remove ribs and seeds for less heat)

1 shallot, cut in small dice

In a medium bowl, whisk together lime juice, oil, garlic, coriander, salt, and paprika. Place the vegetables in the bowl and toss with the marinade. Let the vegetables sit for an hour, stirring occasionally. >

Brazilian Dinner

Pão de queijo

3 tablespoons oil

⅔ cup milk

3 cups/368 grams tapioca starch (if measuring with cups, then spoon the tapioca starch into the cup and level the top with a knife)

1½ teaspoons salt

2 eggs

2 cups shredded Parmesan or sharp cheddar cheese

Butter

Preheat the oven to 375 degrees F. Combine oil and milk and bring to a simmer. Stir together the tapioca starch and salt in the bowl of a stand mixer and pour the hot oil and milk mixture over it. Stir the liquid into the starch and then allow the mixture to cool for 15 minutes. Line a baking sheet with parchment. Beat the eggs into the tapioca mixture and stir in the cheese until it is thoroughly combined. If the dough does not have the texture of playdough, then add additional milk by tablespoons until this texture is achieved. Grease your hands with the butter and roll 1-inch balls of dough. Place these 2 inches apart on the prepared baking sheet. Bake approximately 20–25 minutes or until the rolls are puffed. Keep warm.

1 tablespoon oil

1 onion, cut in ¼-inch dice

3 cloves garlic, pressed or minced

1 (12-ounce) package smoked sausage, cut in ¼-inch dice

2 drops liquid smoke

Place a frying pan over medium heat and add the oil and the onion. Fry the onion until it is translucent. Add the garlic and cook for a few seconds before stirring in the smoked sausage. Fry, stirring frequently, for about 5 minutes. Check beans to make sure they are uniformly tender. Remove any liquid that remains over the surface of the beans until the liquid is at the surface of the beans. Stir the sausage mixture and liquid smoke into the beans. Check seasonings and add additional salt as needed.

Grilled pineapple

Butter or nonstick cooking spray

½ pineapple, peeled and cored

½ cup brown sugar

1 tablespoon water

½ teaspoon salt

¼ teaspoon smoked paprika

Increase oven temperature to 425 degrees F. Grease a rimmed half-sheet pan. Slice the pineapple into ½-inch-thick slices and place on the baking sheet. Bake for 10–15 minutes. Combine the brown sugar, water, salt, and paprika. Turn the pineapple slices over and sprinkle them with the sugar mixture. Bake the pineapple for an additional 10 minutes or until the pineapple is golden.

To serve, place the beans on plates with the pineapple and vegetables on the side. Serve with warm pão de queijo.

 Gluten-Free Variation: This menu is naturally gluten-free.

Homemade Noodle Soup
with Mashed Potatoes and Green Peas

Visiting Grandma-Great in the midst of a true southern Idaho winter was always a treat when I was a little girl. Western Washington had too little snow around the holidays for my taste, and I loved playing outside in the snow and then coming inside for a warm dinner. One of my favorite dinners was homemade noodle soup. After a holiday dinner, Grandma-Great always made homemade noodle soup with the leftover turkey carcass. Despite the images of carnage you may now have in your head, this recipe is a great option for Thanksgiving leftovers. You can use leftover turkey bones and turkey meat or the chicken called for.

The noodles in this recipe are soft, slightly slimy, and rather like long, skinny dumplings. Allowing them to rest helps the gluten to relax so that they're not heavy. However, be careful not to eat too many! The stories of Dad eating too many of these yummy dumpling-like noodles and getting a stomachache are legendary in our family.

Serving the soup over mashed potatoes may seem like starch overload, but just trust me at least once on this. My southern Idaho family serves it this way, and it is yummy. The potatoes, with all of their flavor and creaminess, melt into the chicken stock to further enrich the lovely soup. This is just the dinner for a cold day, though it's not really a good option for a low-carb diet! >

Homemade Noodle Soup with Mashed Potatoes and Green Peas

1 whole chicken	Remove the skin from the top of the chicken and reserve. Cut the breast meat from the rest of the chicken. Cut the breast meat into ¼-inch pieces and refrigerate. Put the chicken frame, neck, legs, and skin into the pot. Add the remaining ingredients and cover everything with cold water. Place over high heat. Reduce the heat to medium-low when bubbles begin to rise to the surface. Skim off foam and discard as it rises to the surface. Cover and simmer for 2–3 hours.
1 turkey wing or drumstick	
1 teaspoon salt	
1 medium onion	
2 carrots	
2 ribs celery	
3 whole cloves garlic, peeled	
1 bay leaf	
1 teaspoon whole peppercorns	
1 teaspoon salt	Whisk the salt into the flour and then stir the eggs into the flour mixture. Add water by tablespoons until the dough comes together in a slightly tacky lump. Generously flour the work surface and roll out the noodle dough until it is 1⅛-inch thick. Use a floured pizza wheel to cut into ¼-inch-wide noodles. Separate the noodles and sprinkle a little flour over them to prevent them from sticking together. Cover the noodles with a clean towel and let sit for at least 30 minutes.
1½ cups flour	
2 eggs, beaten	
Water	
6 medium Yukon Gold potatoes (peeled if you use a regular masher, unpeeled if you use a ricer)	Cut the potatoes into 2-inch chunks and place in a pot of water with garlic cloves. Bring the water to a boil. Boil the potatoes and garlic until they are quite tender, approximately 15 minutes. Drain. Use a potato ricer or masher to break up the potatoes and garlic. Gently fold in the butter, cream, and salt, beginning with ½ teaspoon salt. Taste and adjust your seasonings. Keep warm.
5 large garlic cloves, peeled	
¼ cup butter, softened	
⅓ cup cream	
½ to 1 teaspoon salt	

3 large carrots, peeled and cut in coins	Remove the bones and vegetables from the stock. Use a fat separator or a shallow spoon to remove the fat layer from the top of the stock. Pour the stock into a large bowl and rinse out the pot. Return stock to the pot and put it over medium-high heat, bringing it to a simmer. Add chicken breast, carrots, and noodles and cook until tender, approximately 10 minutes.
1 cup frozen petite green peas	Stir the green peas into the soup and turn off the heat. Adjust seasonings. Serve the soup in individual bowls on top of a mound of potatoes.

Gluten-Free Variation: For gluten-free noodles, combine 1½ cups/213 grams **gluten-free flour blend**, 1 teaspoon **salt**, and 1 teaspoon **xanthan gum** in a large bowl. Break **3 eggs** over the flour mixture and work the eggs into the flour until a smooth dough forms. Roll out the dough on a generously (gluten-free) floured surface and proceed with the recipe as directed above.

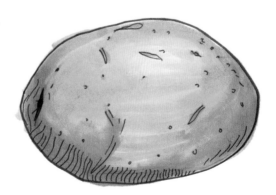

Focaccia-Style Pizza with Greek Salad

When I was growing up, my family went out for pizza at least twice a month. We would go to these old-school pizza places where the atmosphere was permanently perfumed with scents of rich cured meats, toasty cheese, and tangy sauce. It seemed to take so long between when we ordered at the counter up front and when the pizza was delivered to our table. I sat in anticipation on the edge of my vinyl-cushioned seat for my pizza. I liked to eat the crusts with fingers of crispy cheese on them.

In college, I went to Italy with a couple of friends to see the sights and eat the food. On our first night in Rome, quite near the Colosseum,

we tried this style of sheet-pan pizza. I loved the crispy edge and soft center pieces. I said *grazie* and heard *prego* for the first time. I don't remember what toppings covered my pizza, but it's a really great dinner memory anyway, full of the giddiness of being in a new country for the first time.

The gluten-free version of this pizza has been a surprise to many friends who are used to regular all-purpose flour pizza crust. It tastes normal—and people are generally surprised to find that it is gluten-free.

3½ cups/496 grams all-purpose flour 1 cup/142 grams whole wheat flour 1½ teaspoons active dry yeast 1½ teaspoons sugar 1½ teaspoons salt	Line the bottom of a rimmed half-sheet pan with parchment paper or a silicone liner. Whisk ingredients together in the bowl of a heavy-duty stand mixer or in a large bowl.
2½ cups warm water	Stir into the flour mixture. Keep stirring at medium speed for 5–8 minutes, or until the dough becomes elastic. Spread this dough into the prepared baking sheet and cover with an inverted rimmed half-sheet pan. Place the dough in the refrigerator to rise for approximately 5 hours (if you have time)—this will produce a more complex flavor—or at room temperature for about 45 minutes. Prick the risen dough all over with a fork to reduce bubbling.
2 tablespoons olive oil ½ teaspoon coarse sea salt	Preheat the oven to 425 degrees F. Drizzle the olive oil over the top of the dough and brush lightly to distribute it evenly. Sprinkle evenly with the sea salt. Once the oven is ready, bake the dough for 15 minutes.
1 cup marinara sauce 16 ounces shredded mozzarella cheese, divided ¼ cup grated Parmesan cheese ½ teaspoon sea salt *Other toppings* (choose up to 3) 1 cup sliced pepperoni or ham 1 cup well-drained pineapple tidbits ¼ cup pesto ½ cup chopped caramelized onions ¼ cup chopped black olives	Spread the sauce evenly on top of the crust. Sprinkle with half of the mozzarella cheese. Add desired toppings. Sprinkle with the remaining mozzarella and Parmesan cheeses. Sprinkle with sea salt. Return to the oven and bake an additional 5–7 minutes, or until everything is melty and browning. Allow the pizza to sit for a couple of minutes before removing it from the pan and cutting it into rectangles. ›

Focaccia-Style Pizza with Greek Salad

1 head romaine lettuce ½ cup Kalamata olives 2 ounces feta cheese 1 cup grape tomatoes 1 medium cucumber	While the pizza is cooking, wash and dry the lettuce and tear it into 2- to 3-inch pieces. Quarter the olives, crumble the cheese, slice the tomatoes in half, and peel and cut the cucumber into pieces the same size as the tomatoes. Add all of these ingredients to a large salad bowl.
½ cup good olive oil 3 tablespoons red wine vinegar 1 teaspoon sugar ½ teaspoon salt ½ teaspoon oregano ½ teaspoon freshly ground pepper	In a small bowl whisk together the oil, vinegar, sugar, salt, oregano, and pepper. Just before serving the salad, drizzle this dressing on the top of the salad and toss to coat evenly. Taste for salt and pepper and adjust seasonings before serving.

Gluten-Free Variation: Combine ½ cup warm **water**, 4 teaspoons **yeast**, and 1½ teaspoons **sugar** in a cup. In a large bowl, whisk together 1 cup/114 grams **tapioca starch**, ¾ cup/127 grams **potato starch**, 1½ cups/213 grams **gluten-free flour blend**, 1 cup/138 grams **garbanzo bean flour**, ⅓ cup **sugar**, 2 teaspoons **xanthan gum**, and 1 teaspoon **salt**. Pour **yeast mixture**, ½ cup **oil**, and 1⅔ cup warm **water** into the flour mixture. Stir for 5–6 minutes. Spread dough into a parchment-lined rimmed half-sheet pan and allow the dough to rise for 45 minutes to 1 hour. Bake as directed above. This batter (it is really too loose to be called a dough) can also be used to make traditional round pizza pies. You will need a pizza stone or flat metal baking sheet, a pizza peel or additional flat metal baking sheet, and parchment paper. Tear off 3 approximately 13-inch-square pieces of parchment paper. Take approximately one-third of the batter and place it in the middle of one of the sheets of parchment. Use a spatula (offset is great for this) to spread the batter into a 12-inch circle that is thin in the center and thicker around the edges. Repeat with remaining dough and parchment. Allow the pizza to rise for 30–45 minutes. Preheat the oven with the stone/baking sheet on the oven rack for 20 minutes. Slide the peel or flat baking sheet under the parchment and transfer it to the hot stone. Bake for 8–10 minutes, until the crust is golden in places. Remove the pizza crust from the oven using the peel and add desired toppings. Bake an additional 5 minutes to finish the pizza.

Thai-Style Noodles with Cucumber Salad, Sticky Rice, and Peanut Sauce

My first experience with pad thai was one of those wonderful defining moments for my palate. Some college friends invited me to a Thai restaurant for dinner. Although I'd grown up with Japanese food and other Asian foods, I had never before tried Thai cuisine. At the restaurant, I was greeted with a unique bouquet that was at once distinguishable and yet wonderfully melded together. Only later would I learn that these smells were fish sauce, curry paste, palm sugar, and tamarind. My friends ordered a family-style dinner, and I reveled in the savory sweetness of pad thai and discovered a new comfort food in red pineapple curry. The sticky rice balls dipped in peanut sauce intrigued me as they took the place of rolls and butter but were so different! In subsequent visits, I wanted to try different dishes, but it was also hard to get beyond the pad thai.

My first attempt at making a Thai dinner resulted in dinner much later than usual. I went shopping with Kleine in Seattle's International District to find the tamarind, sticky rice, and curry paste. We got lost—and inspired—amid the mysterious labels and intriguing smells of those narrow little shops. I wished so badly that I could read the labels and ask about them. When we finally made it home with our bounty and began prepping, we realized that we had embarked on an adventure that was going to require a lot of learning and lots of chopping. It was so good in the end, though. >

Thai-Style Noodles with Cucumber Salad, Sticky Rice, and Peanut Sauce

Prep Time: overnight + 1 hour · *Cook Time:* 45 minutes · *Total Time:* 25 hours, 45 minutes

2 cups glutinous rice	Place the rice in a bowl and cover with water. Soak 6–8 hours.
Cucumber relish ¼ cup sugar ½ teaspoon salt 1 tablespoon rice vinegar 1 teaspoon water ¼ teaspoon chili flakes 1 English cucumber, quartered and diced	Combine everything but the cucumber and bring to a simmer, stirring constantly, until the sugar is just dissolved and sauce is clear. Pour the syrup over the cucumber pieces. Stir cucumbers periodically to ensure that the cucumbers are evenly coated.
Peanut sauce 1 cup coconut milk 1 teaspoon to 1 tablespoon red curry paste, to taste ⅓ cup peanut butter 3 tablespoons palm sugar 2 tablespoons fish sauce 2 tablespoons fresh lime juice (1 lime=2 tablespoons juice)	Spoon a tablespoon of the thick cream at the top of the coconut milk into a saucepan over medium heat. Stir in the curry paste and cook, stirring constantly, for about 45 seconds. Add more chili paste if you want a spicier sauce. Whisk in the remaining ingredients, including the rest of the coconut milk, until the sugar is dissolved and everything is combined. Simmer to thicken. Taste and adjust the seasonings.
Pad thai sauce ⅓ cup lime juice (3 limes=⅓ cup juice) ⅔ cup palm sugar ¼ cup fish sauce 1 tablespoon red curry paste ¼ cup vegetable oil	Whisk together and set aside.

Tip: The sticky (or glutinous rice) takes some planning to add to this menu, but it is well worth seeking out and taking the time to soak. My whole family loves sticky rice—possibly because it breaks the rule of not playing with our food. They all use their fingers to roll it into little balls before eating it. Also, do try to find the palm sugar. The difference in flavor is noticeable. You can also make this with brown sugar, but doing so will produce a pad thai that isn't as good as what you're hoping to create.

Soaked rice	Pour about 1 inch of water into the bottom of a large saucepan. Put a metal steaming basket into the pan. Line it with a smooth (not terry cloth) dish towel. Spoon the sticky rice into the dish towel. Cover the pot and wrap the ends of the cloth over the pot cover. Place the pot over high heat until you begin to see steam, then reduce the heat to maintain a simmer. Simmer approximately 20 minutes, then turn off the heat, keeping the rice covered.
1 (10-ounce) package pad thai rice noodles	Cover the noodles with hot water and set aside for 15–20 minutes until the noodles are nice and pliable.
1 tablespoon vegetable oil 12–16 ounces raw large shrimp, thawed and shelled	Heat a large sauté pan over medium-high heat. Add the oil when the pan is hot. Place half the shrimp in the pan. Cook without turning for 1 minute. Turn the shrimp and cook for an additional minute or until the shrimp turn pinkish and curl. Move the cooked shrimp to a bowl and repeat with remaining shrimp. Drain the noodles.
1 tablespoon oil 1 medium shallot or green onion, minced ¼ tablespoon salt 3 garlic cloves, pressed 3 eggs, beaten	Add the oil, the shallots, and salt to the hot pan. Stir-fry for a minute. Add the garlic and count to 20 while stirring constantly. Add eggs to pan and stir-fry until they are cooked. Set the cooked eggs aside with the shrimp.
Garnishes ¼ cup roasted peanuts, chopped coarsely ½ small cucumber, peeled and cut into ⅛-inch matchsticks ¼ cup cilantro, chopped coarsely 10 fresh chives, chopped lime wedges	Add the noodles to the pan. Pour the pad thai sauce over the noodles. Toss the noodles with tongs to coat them evenly and allow the noodles to absorb the sauce and get soft. Return the meat and eggs to the pan and toss to combine. Top with garnishes and serve immediately with a wedge of lime.

 Gluten-Free Variation: This menu is naturally gluten-free.

Moroccan-Style Chickpea Stew
with Bread and Preserved Lemon Salsa

We have a family tradition of having an around-the-world dinner to celebrate New Year's Eve. We generally begin with appetizers from Asia and work our way west. My kids, perhaps wowed with excitement and the fancy dinner served in courses, will sit through the long dinner and even eat foods that might be considered gross any other day. This Moroccan-style stew, or tagine, was a dish that made its debut at a New Year's dinner.

Chickpeas came into my consciousness when I moved to Spokane, Washington, several years ago. Spokane is on the edge of the Palouse, a hilly region of eastern Washington and northern Idaho, whose climate and soil are just right for growing chickpeas and other legumes. As I have experimented beyond their most common use in hummus, I have come to love them. Their darling shape really looks like a tiny chick, all fluffed out and round. Their substantial size gives them a satisfactory presence in dishes where meat would generally be featured.

Chickpeas are wonderfully suited for a tagine, a hearty stew from Morocco traditionally cooked in a special peaked pot and served with a variety of accompaniments that provide interesting flavor and textural counterpoints. The preserved lemon salsa is amazing on its own and, when paired with the crispy, salty fried onions, brings this dish together in a very satisfying way. If you cannot find preserved lemons to purchase, make your own with the recipe here, but be aware that it will take a week for them to preserve.

(Begin one week ahead)

6 medium organic lemons

5 to 6 tablespoons salt

Pint jar

Wash the lemons well. Cut three lemons into wedges that are ½-inch thick at the widest part of the peel. Wash and dry the jar. Add 1 tablespoon of salt to the bottom of the jar. Pour 3 tablespoons of salt on a plate. Dredge each lemon wedge on both sides with salt. Pack the lemons in the jar. Use an additional tablespoon of salt if necessary to dredge all the lemon wedges. Pour the remaining tablespoon of salt over the lemons. Juice the remaining three lemons and pour the juice over the lemon wedges in the jar. Screw the lid on the jar securely and place on the kitchen counter. Turn the jar over twice daily. The lemons will be ready in a week. After they have cured, store them in the refrigerator.

(Begin the night before if possible)

6 cups water

1 pound dried chickpeas

1 teaspoon salt

Pick through the chickpeas to remove any broken or shriveled beans. Add them to a large bowl and cover with water. Stir in the salt. Soak overnight. Alternatively, quick soak them by bringing the chickpeas to a boil for two minutes. Add the salt, take them off the heat, and cover them, allowing them to soak for an hour.

(Begin the night before if possible)

Bread

3 cups/425 grams all-purpose flour

1 cup/142 grams whole wheat flour

1 teaspoon salt

1½ teaspoons yeast

¼ cup honey

¼ cup olive oil

1 cup water

Whisk together the flours, salt, and yeast. Whisk together the honey, oil, and water. Stir the oil mixture into the flour until universally moistened. Cover the dough and place it in the refrigerator to rise overnight. >

2 bay leaves	Rinse the soaked beans and add them to a large Dutch oven. Cover with 2 inches of water. Add the bay leaves. Bring the chickpeas to a simmer (a few bubbles breaking the surface), cover, then simmer for 2½ hours, or until the beans are tender and the water is level with the beans.
1 onion, peeled ⅔ cup oil ¼ cup flour Salt	Slice the onion in half from the stem to the root. Cut along the ridges into slices that are as thin as you can make them. Heat the oil in a large saucepan over medium heat. When hot, dredge the onions in the flour and add them to the oil in 4 batches. Fry until golden and drain on paper towels. Sprinkle with salt.
2 tablespoons chopped preserved lemon peel 4 fresh figs 2 shallots 1 (6–8 inch) cucumber 4–6 leaves mint 2 teaspoons lemon juice ½ teaspoon salt	Remove any seeds from the lemon and chop the peel and pulp into small pieces. Stem the figs and chop them into ¼-inch dice. Chop shallots into ¼-inch pieces. Chop cucumber into ½-inch dice. Mince mint leaves. Stir ingredients together with lemon juice and salt. Allow flavors to meld for a few minutes and taste. Add additional salt to taste.
Bread baking Flour	Turn dough out onto a lightly floured surface and divide it in half. Form each half into a ½-inch-thick circle. Cover and let rise 1 hour. Preheat the oven to 425 degrees F. Place a baking sheet into the oven while it is preheating. Cut a cross into the top of each loaf. Pull the hot pan out of the oven and dust it with a bit of flour. Place each round on the sheet and bake 20–25 minutes.

Finishing tagine

1 tablespoon olive oil

½ onion, chopped

2 carrots, peeled and chopped

¼ teaspoon salt

1 (14-ounce) can chopped tomatoes with juice

½ teaspoon ground coriander

2 tablespoons fish sauce

Add oil to a Dutch oven over medium heat. Add the onion, carrots, and salt. Cook until the onion and carrots are tender. Stir in the tomatoes and coriander. Add the cooked beans with bean stock and fish sauce. Simmer uncovered for 30–35 minutes to allow flavors to meld. Taste and adjust seasonings. Serve with bread, lemon salsa, and fried onions.

Gluten-Free Variation: Make **gluten-free bread**. Whisk together in a small bowl ¼ cup warm water, 1 tablespoon **sugar**, and 1 tablespoon **active dry yeast**. Whisk together in a large bowl 1½ cups/213 grams **gluten-free flour blend**, ½ cup/86 grams **potato starch**, ½ cup/65 grams **tapioca starch**, 1 cup/138 grams **garbanzo bean flour**, 2 teaspoons **xanthan gum**, and 1 teaspoon **salt**. Whisk together in a small bowl 2 **eggs**, ½ cup **oil**, 1 cup **warm water**, and ½ cup **sugar**. Add the egg mixture to the flour mixture. Stir the yeast mixture into the dough. Mix for 5–7 minutes until the dough becomes really thick, sticky, and uniform. Cover and let rest for 20 minutes. Line a baking sheet with parchment paper. Dampen your hands with water and take about ⅓ of the dough, placing the mound on the parchment, and lightly pat it into a circular shape. Smooth the top with your damp hands. Repeat with the remaining dough. Sift **gluten-free flour** over the loaves and make decorative cuts on the top if you desire. Do not cover the dough. Allow it to rise for about 45–60 minutes. After the dough has been rising for about 30 minutes, preheat the oven to 350 degrees F. When the dough is done rising, bake it for approximately 30 minutes until the interior temperature reaches 200 degrees F. Cool before slicing.

Use **garbanzo bean flour** to coat the **onions** before frying.

This cookbook project has been in the works for several years, and it has evolved in its scope and premise during this time. When Hervor was little, she decided she wanted to write a cookbook, too, so I proposed an idea. It involved fun poems to accompany various dishes that were appealing to children. Hervor was going to illustrate it. While we did not finish that cookbook, one little poem has stuck in my mind ever since:

> Do you like your vegetables?
> "No!" you say. "They're gross-ted!"
> If you dislike your vegetables,
> You haven't tried them roasted!

It is true that roasted vegetables can be a great way for children to get used to the idea of cooked vegetables. Despite the fact that they often push back, there is a lot of wisdom in persevering and just requiring one bite. After quite a while, my kids have gotten more interested in vegetables. Although they still prefer raw vegetables over cooked most of the time, they also—particularly Nancy D—have begun to appreciate the caramelized delights of cooked vegetables. The following are a few of my favorites.

Accompaniments

MOSTLY VEGETABLES
10 to 40 Minutes Total

Sweet Onion Green Beans

If you treat frozen vegetables correctly, they can be an excellent time-saver. Frozen vegetables are blanched before they're frozen. This deactivates an enzyme that would otherwise cause the vegetable to break down even while they are frozen. Blanching involves cooking the vegetables briefly before quickly freezing them. It means that the frozen vegetables you buy are half-cooked already, and they do not need much more cooking to be perfect. Make sure to not overdo the reheating, and you will be rewarded with great results and very easy preparation. This is particularly true of green beans, which always seem to take a great deal of trimming.

1 pound frozen green beans	Place beans into a bowl of cold water to defrost them.
2 tablespoons oil 1 large onion, chopped ½ teaspoon salt	Place a large skillet over medium-high heat. Add the oil; when it is hot, add the onion and salt and cook, stirring occasionally, until the onions become translucent and slightly browned on the edges. This will take approximately 5 minutes.
2 tablespoons brown sugar 1 tablespoon whole grain Dijon mustard 1 tablespoon water	Whisk together and stir into the onions. Remove from heat.
	Drain the beans well. Add the beans to the onions and sauté briefly until the beans are just heated through. Salt and pepper to taste.

 **Gluten-Free Variation:** This recipe is naturally gluten-free.

Marinated Kale Salad

I love digging in the dirt and having a pretty garden—I even like to weed most of the time—but I have never been particularly successful with vegetables, mostly because my family often goes on vacation in July, and a week or two without great attention and care isn't ideal for vegetable gardens. I often hope that someday I will manage a good vegetable garden, and when I do, I will grow lacinato kale for this salad.

¼ cup olive oil 3 tablespoons lemon juice 1 large garlic clove, pressed or minced ¼ teaspoon salt 1 tablespoon Dijon mustard ¼ teaspoon freshly ground pepper	Whisk together in a large bowl.
1 bunch lacinato kale	Remove stems and cut kale into ½-inch ribbons. Stir into the olive oil marinade and allow the kale to sit for at least 30 minutes.
3 tablespoons sunflower seeds ⅓ cup dried sweetened cranberries	Mix into the salad prior to serving.

Gluten-Free Variation: This recipe is naturally gluten-free.

Roasted Cauliflower with Thyme

There is something that almost feels like cheating when it comes to roasted vegetables. For one thing, they are so simple to make. For another, the roasting brings all of the vegetables' natural sugars to the fore while tempering the bitterness that sometimes turns people off. Add oil and salt, and the result is almost better than dessert. *Almost.* I have to watch the pans of roasted vegetables at my house, or Nancy D and I will snack them away before dinner even begins! Cauliflower is a favorite vegetable roast. I love the addition of thyme, both for the flavor it lends as well as the color it brings to the otherwise monochromatic cauliflower.

5 cups cauliflower florets 3 tablespoons oil	Preheat the oven to 450 degrees F. Toss the cauliflower and oil together. Spread out onto a rimmed half-sheet pan.
¾ to 1 teaspoon salt 2 teaspoons fresh thyme leaves	Sprinkle cauliflower with salt and thyme. Roast for 15 minutes and stir to turn the vegetables over. Roast for 5 additional minutes or until the cauliflower is soft and caramelized on the edges. Adjust the seasonings and serve hot or warm.

Gluten-Free Variation: This recipe is naturally gluten-free.

Green Pea Salad

As I was growing up, my life was punctuated by the growing seasons of peas and corn, which were the two principal crops for my family's frozen food business. Dad worked tirelessly to keep the business going, and peas were a staple in our dinners. During pea and corn harvest, Dad made many trips across the Cascade Mountains to visit the production plant in central Washington. On lucky days, Kleine and I got to join him and spend the day with our cousins. Those were lovely golden summer days full of backyard play, pie, and home-churned ice cream. This pea salad is a great option for summertime barbecues!

1 (16-ounce) package frozen petite green peas 1 (8-ounce) can water chestnuts, chopped	Add the peas to a medium saucepan and add enough water to just cover the peas. Bring to a simmer and drain the peas immediately. Combine the peas and water chestnuts in a large bowl.
10 slices bacon 1 cup shredded sharp cheddar cheese	Cook the bacon until crisp. Allow to cool, and chop. Combine the cheese and bacon and set aside.
3 tablespoons mayonnaise 3 tablespoons plain yogurt or sour cream ½ teaspoon smoked paprika Salt to taste	Combine ingredients. Taste and season with salt. Toss the pea and mayonnaise mixtures together. Immediately before serving stir in the cheese and bacon mixture.

Gluten-Free Variation: This recipe is naturally gluten-free.

Breakfast often makes me think of Kleine. When we were little girls, she was the one who liked breakfast, and I was the one who would rather just skip to lunch. While bacon was tolerable, and a good dipping egg and toast were both fascinating and delicious enough for me to feel like eating, it was years before I discovered the appeal of many breakfast staples such as pancakes, waffles, and French toast. At some point my dislike of breakfast foods changed, and I began to appreciate breakfast for what it is.

Now I find that opinions are polarized in my family about breakfast. I try to offer my children a little grace as I remember how breakfast was often difficult for me, but I do hope and smile a little as Dr. Lu refuses to eat French toast, Nancy D declares waffles disgusting, Bear will eat only said waffles and pancakes with peanut butter under the syrup, and Hervor declares she is sick of waffles and pancakes and lobbies for French toast. To each his or her own, I guess. Unless they take the responsibility of making breakfast, they do have to live with the one I make! These sorts of reactions often lead to the rather tired conversation about how we need to eat not just to be delighted by the food but also to be physically sustained by it. There is a balance to strike between mere sustenance and honoring individual favorites when one is cooking for a family. In the end, being "hangry" is not a good thing for any of us, particularly when we meet with the inevitable frustrations that come up every day. Around here, some breakfast—any breakfast—is an essential step away from hangry. Here are some of our favorites.

Breakfast

HERE WE GO AGAIN!
25 to 40 Minutes Total

Crunchy Granola Bars

Crunchy granola bars are great for breakfast on the way out the door. I generally do not make these on weekday mornings because they take some time to cool, so I have to hide them on Saturday if I want them to stick around long enough for breakfasts the next week. These are a great snack for hikes and other outdoor activities as well.

2 cups rolled oats 1 cup granulated sugar 1 cup nuts 1 cup unsweetened coconut	Preheat the oven to 425 degrees F. Line a rimmed half-sheet pan with a silicone liner or parchment. Pulverize ingredients in a food processor or blender. Place powdered oat mixture in a large bowl.
3 cups rolled oats	Stir into the oat mixture.
½ cup oil ¼ cup honey 1 teaspoon salt ½ teaspoon baking soda 1 teaspoon almond extract 1 teaspoon vanilla extract ¼ cup water Butter or nonstick cooking spray	Whisk together everything but the butter or non-stick cooking spray and pour over the oat mixture. Stir to thoroughly combine. Pour this mixture into the prepared pan and spread it evenly out to the edges. Grease the outside bottom of a second rimmed half-sheet pan. Nest this baking sheet over the oat mixture. Place a large saucepan with a lid on the top baking sheet. Lean heavily on the saucepan lid while moving the pan evenly over the sheet pan to thoroughly compress the oat mixture.. Remove the top baking sheet. Bake the bars for 15–20 minutes. Rotate the pan halfway through the baking time to prevent burning the honey. Cool slightly and then cut into bars (a bench scraper works well for this). Cool in the pan until the cut bars are firm.

Gluten-Free Variation: Make sure to use **gluten-free oats**.

Granola

Shortly before I began law school, I flew to a good friend's house in California and then drove back to college with her so that she didn't have to drive alone. It was a fun trip to a new part of the world that I had never seen before. The town she was from was nestled in heavily forested mountains, and it seemed like the perfect setting for enjoying my first taste of homemade granola. And I sure did enjoy it. I loved the salty-sweet oats with the crunchy nuts and seeds. There were raisins in the granola as well, and I, a raisin fan, enjoyed the chewy texture they brought to the bite. It all felt so healthy to eat, and it was so much better than premade, store-bought granola.

Later, after I married Mr. Kent, I made him granola regularly on weekends until Saturday mornings became more complicated with kids. Now it's an occasional treat. I still love the toasty goodness of granola when I can get around to making it!

Butter or nonstick cooking spray 8 cups/709 grams rolled oats 2 cups roasted nut pieces 2 cups coconut flakes ¼ cup roasted sunflower seeds ½ cup roasted pepitas	Preheat oven to 300 degrees F. Grease two rimmed half-sheet pans. Combine ingredients in a large bowl.
1 cup sugar ½ cup oil ½ cup honey or maple syrup 1½ teaspoons salt	Combine ingredients in a medium pot. Bring to a boil, stirring frequently, and boil one minute.
1 teaspoon vanilla extract 1 teaspoon almond extract	Stir ingredients into the syrup mixture. Pour the syrup over the oat mixture and stir to coat everything thoroughly. This will take a minute or two. Spread the mixture evenly on the two baking sheets and place in the top third and bottom third of the oven. Bake for 10–15 minutes before removing, stirring, and rotating the pans so that the one that was on the top is now on the bottom. Bake an additional 10–15 minutes. Check for overbrowning.
1 cup raisins, optional	Add the raisins if desired, then bake an additional 5–10 minutes. Cool completely and store in an airtight container.

Gluten-Free Variation: Make sure to use **gluten-free oats**.

Waffles

Despite the fact that I did not particularly appreciate waffles and pancakes as a little girl, I didn't mind waffle weekend too much, because it was fascinating to watch Dad prepare his waffles. He would intentionally place a small piece of butter into each waffle pocket, pick up the pitcher of warmed syrup (Mom always warmed her syrup), swirl it slightly to break up any skin that might have formed on top of the syrup, and pour the syrup over the whole. Once I learned to like waffles, I found that a bit of melty butter in each pocket was the perfect way to eat them.

3 cups/425 grams all-purpose flour

4 teaspoons baking powder

½ teaspoon baking soda

⅓ cup sugar

1 teaspoon salt

Preheat the waffle iron. Whisk together ingredients in a large bowl.

2 cups milk

4 eggs

⅔ cup oil

Whisk together in a medium bowl, then pour over flour mixture and whisk just until the flour is uniformly moistened. Some small lumps may remain. Pour batter onto hot waffle iron and cook according to manufacturer's instructions. Leftover waffles can be frozen for a quick weekday breakfast.

Gluten-Free Variation: Combine 3 cups/425 grams **gluten-free flour blend**, 4 teaspoons **baking powder**, ½ teaspoon **baking soda**, ¼ teaspoon **xanthan gum**, 1 teaspoon **salt**, and ⅓ cup **sugar**. Whisk together 4 **eggs** and ½ cup **oil** until smooth. Whisk in 1½ cups **milk** and 1 cup **Greek yogurt**. Whisk the milk mixture into the flour mixture until it is very smooth. Cook on a preheated nonstick (but uncontaminated with wheat) waffle iron. These waffles will seem to stick on the waffle iron but can easily be pried off by slipping the edge of a flat spatula along the edge of the waffle and pulling it up.

Poached Eggs on English Muffins

Weekday mornings are always kind of a rush during the school year despite every good intention to be early and not rushed. Inevitably there seems to be a lost book or a forgotten form to fill out or, frankly, a newspaper interesting enough to distract me from the schedule. Too often we end up with less sustaining breakfasts that necessitate a snack before 10 a.m. I do try to insist on protein, like peanut butter and honey toast (yum!) or poached eggs on toast or rice. Poached eggs on toast is one of Hervor and Nancy D's favorite breakfast requests. Sometimes it's even useful in convincing a reluctant teenager to get out of bed and ready for school. I can put it together in just about the time it takes my kiddos to get dressed and brush their hair.

Poached eggs are one of the world's great simple foods. They require minimal preparation, create their own luscious sauce, and taste great with a simple application of salt. When paired with hot buttered toast, poached eggs elevate potentially less interesting breakfast fare, such as toast or plain rice, to something wonderful and highly satisfactory. The better the eggs, the better the result. I like pastured eggs best.

4 English muffins 4 tablespoons butter	Split the muffins. Toast, butter, and keep warm.
2–3 pieces of fruit	Cut and arrange on a serving plate.
1 tablespoon distilled white vinegar 8 eggs	Fill a large saucepan ⅔ full of water. Add the vinegar and bring to a simmer. Crack one egg at a time into a small bowl. Slide the egg into the water and repeat with up to 2–3 more eggs. The number of eggs will depend on the size of your pan, but each cooking egg should have an inch or so of simmering water around it. Poach eggs for approximately 2–3 minutes or until the whites are set and the yolks are still soft. Remove the eggs with a slotted spoon and allow them to drain briefly before placing them on buttered muffins. Serve immediately with ketchup or salt and pepper.

Gluten-Free Variation: Use good **gluten-free bread** or English muffins for the toast.

BREAKFAST

The first food I remember making all by myself was a batch of cutout sugar cookies. I was so excited about my solo baking, and I know that Mom tried to be enthusiastic, but the mess in her kitchen was a little hard to deal with. She would still tell you the story if you asked her—all of that flour everywhere left a lasting impression. Flour—especially when mingled with wet, sticky things like eggs—is tough to clean up because it basically turns into glue. As we moved forward, and I began to share her kitchen more and more, she tried to teach me about cleaning up as I went along. She taught me to read and follow a recipe, and she gave me space to develop this interest, though it was certainly inconvenient for her. That is what great moms do! I work to remember her example when Nancy D and Hervor ask to bake by themselves. I know the mess is coming, but I try to keep Mom's long-range view and let them go for it. Baking is part of our family culture, and I just love it.

The baking section is also the first place I turn when I begin browsing a new cookbook. As I read these recipes, I can almost feel the paradoxically sticky but satiny bread dough, smell the warmth of toasted flour and butter, and taste the sweet alchemy that is cookie dough. Sweet and savory baking is at the heart of a welcoming kitchen. If you are a person who is a little less comfortable with baking, purchase a kitchen scale, look for a book with good descriptions and weight measures (ounces or grams) for flour—and don't forget the salt.

Baking and Candy

COMFORT AND MAGIC

Quick Breads

If you are new to baking, quick breads are the easiest place to begin. Rather than dealing with gluten development and yeast, which can be kind of intimidating, quick breads rely on rapidly bringing a basic dough together that will rely on a very dependable chemical reaction to rise. Remember the grade school volcanoes with the little cup in the top for sodium bicarbonate (i.e., baking soda), over which vinegar would be poured to create lots of foamy "lava"? This is the same reaction that puffs up quick breads. No proofing or kneading are required. Because you can bake your breads immediately, it means that you will be enjoying your baking in mere minutes rather than hours!

Yeast Breads

Yeast is a great divider between hard-core home bakers and dabblers. This shouldn't really be surprising when you consider that the divide exists even in professional French baking, where there is patisserie—the cakes and pastries—and there is boulangerie—the yeasted breads. It is easy to understand this divide, since there are so many idiosyncrasies with both styles, but don't let this dissuade you from trying your own bread. Not every recipe is complicated. Yeast is more forgiving than you may think. Just be careful to not heat things up too quickly, let the dough take its time, and you will be fine. Even kneading is optional these days with a rustic bread approach. If your schedule does not allow for fresh bread all the time (and really, whose does?), it is still worth giving this skill a little place in the culinary part of your brain. Doesn't the idea of smelling freshly baked bread and slathering melting butter on a still slightly warm roll seem to make it worth a try?

Wheat flour works with yeast in interesting ways—particularly in the development of gluten—to produce the springy and soft bread that many of us are used to. While gluten-free yeast-risen doughs are much looser and can be difficult to work with, they are also not impossible. When, as a result of a celiac or wheat allergy diagnosis, one faces a future devoid of doughnuts or dinner breads, it is good to embrace the possible and learn to roll with the differences.

Breads

30 Minutes to 8 Hours

Gluten-Free Flour Blend

Mr. Kent has been my biggest cheerleader in my gluten-free journey. With pride in his voice, he tells people that I make good gluten-free baked goods, and that I have my own flour blend. It's affirming to have him cheer me on instead of complaining that they taste different. There have been many twists and turns in the road that led to this flour blend and these recipes. I am so thankful that he never complained about the early versions of a recipe and so grateful that my family persisted with me until I got these recipes right!

When I make gluten-free bakes, I use my own gluten-free flour blend to reduce costs, regulate xanthan gum levels, and utilize the power of garbanzo bean flour. Most commercially available gluten-free flour blends will work in these recipes. Blends with a starch listed as the first ingredient rather than a gritty flour (such as rice or millet) are not adequate substitutes. You may want to reduce the amount of xanthan gum if your blend already contains xanthan gum.

This flour blend is unique in its inclusion of garbanzo flour. Gluten-free baking really came together for me after I discovered the power of the bean! The gritty flours (rice and sorghum) provide bulk and structure, while the starches provide springiness and loft. Garbanzo has a little of both and brings the whole thing together nicely with some added binding power. Don't worry about the beany odor of the unbaked batters or doughs. This will bake away and not be noticed in the final product. If you find you like this blend, make more than one batch, and then you can avoid making a huge mess of your kitchen every week or so.

Be patient with yourself in your journey. Things will feel, look, and smell a little different, but keep the faith in the process. You can enjoy baked goods without gluten, and your family can enjoy great baked goods without you worrying about cross-contamination in the kitchen.

4 cups/560 grams brown rice flour 3 cups/461 grams sorghum flour	Whisk together thoroughly.
2 cups/372 grams potato starch 1 cup/137 grams tapioca starch 1½ cups/198 grams garbanzo flour	Whisk into the flour blend. Store in an airtight container.

Biscuits for Dinner or Shortcake

When I was growing up, my parents both worked. Mom was a high school English teacher and Dad had a frozen food company. They were both so busy with work and taking care of us that it amazes me that we ate so many homemade dinners. On occasion, however, we got to eat fast food. Mom opted for fried chicken on the night we got lost in the foggy woods on the way home from visiting a friend. During this pre–cell phone era adventure, Mom, Kleine, and I were all sure we would run out of gas and have to spend the night in the woods with the wild animals. We all prayed that Mom would find her way out, and, after a couple of hours, she did! We were all so excited to get back into town and see the red and white lights of the Kentucky Fried Chicken franchise. While I liked the chicken, my favorite menu item was the biscuits. These were the first biscuits I really remember eating. I loved their delightfully fluffy texture.

These biscuits are lovely. They are a great quick breakfast with butter and jam, or a nice accompaniment to dinner. I cut the biscuits into squares, rather than the traditional circles, to reduce handling the dough and promote lightness in the biscuits. You can also use the dough to make a quick pan of cinnamon buns without having to wait for the dough to rise.

3 cups/425 grams all-purpose flour 3 tablespoons baking powder 1 teaspoon salt ½ cup sugar (optional—add for shortcakes or sweet biscuits)	Preheat the oven to 350 degrees F. Whisk ingredients together.
½ cup/96 grams shortening	Rub into the flour mixture with your hands until the flour mixture resembles damp sand in the way it holds together and falls apart. There should be no large pieces of shortening.
¾ cup milk ½ cup plain yogurt	Whisk together. Pour over flour mixture and cut liquid into the flour mixture with a spatula. When no dry spots remain, turn the mixture out onto a lightly floured surface and pat into a rough square. Fold the left side over in half and press down. Repeat with the top, right side, and bottom. Roll the square into a 9x13-inch rectangle. Use a floured pizza wheel to cut the dough into four horizontal rows and six vertical rows. Place on a baking sheet and bake for 20 minutes.

Gluten-Free Variation: Preheat the oven to 425 degrees F. Combine in a large bowl 2½ cups/354 grams **gluten-free flour blend**, 2 tablespoons + 1 teaspoon **baking powder**, ½ teaspoon **salt**, and 1 teaspoon **xanthan gum**. Add ½ cup **sugar** if you are making shortcakes or sweet biscuits. Cut ½ cup/114 grams cold **butter** into small pieces. Rub the butter into the flour mixture with your hands until the mixture resembles crumbly damp sand. Whisk together ¾ cup **milk** and ½ cup **plain yogurt**. Pour the yogurt mixture over the flour and stir together until thoroughly combined—one nice thing about working with gluten-free quick breads is that you will never have overdeveloped gluten and tough bakes! Work 1½ cups shredded **sharp cheese** into the dough if desired. Generously flour a work surface with **gluten-free flour**. Pat the dough into a 1-inch-thick rectangle. Use a bench scraper or flat metal spatula to remove the dough if it sticks to your work surface. Cut the dough into individual pieces using a pizza cutter or knife. Place the biscuits onto a greased or parchment-lined baking tray. Bake for 15-20 minutes or until the biscuits are golden on top. Cool slightly before serving.

Gluten-Free Almond Poppy Seed Muffins

I *first came* to love poppy seed bakes as a little girl when I ate my babysitter's poppy seed Bundt cake. She used a yellow cake mix, and I loved it. Later, when my family got a membership at Costco, my mom purchased the huge poppy seed muffins that were sold by the dozen. Kleine and I loved eating them warmed up in the microwave and slathered with margarine (I know, butter would have been better, but we had cholesterol issues and the doctor recommended margarine, so there you are). I have no idea how many calories we consumed in those little "snacks." I am sure I would think twice now, but as a very active nine-year-old it didn't matter much to me.

These muffins were one of the first hopeful stops in my gluten-free journey. In a moment when I was feeling both relieved to have found the cause of my issues and uncertain how to proceed into this strange world of alternative flours, I remembered poppy seed muffins and tried to make them. Success! The muffins were yummy. The muffins were normal. The muffins did not taste in the least bit gluten-free. They were a step in the right direction. With this recipe, I may even be able to re-create a childhood memory if I buy some giant muffin tins and margarine. Well, maybe just the tins!

Butter or nonstick cooking spray

2½ cups/354 grams gluten-free flour blend

¾ cup granulated sugar

2 teaspoons baking powder

½ teaspoon baking soda

½ teaspoon salt

1 tablespoon poppy seeds

½ teaspoon xanthan gum

Preheat the oven to 350 degrees F. Grease 2 standard (12-cup) muffin tins. Whisk dry ingredients together in a medium bowl.

---

3 eggs

½ cup oil

⅔ cup milk

¾ cup Greek yogurt

1 teaspoon vanilla extract

1 teaspoon almond extract

Whisk together until the mixture is smooth. Stir in the flour mixture until it is completely incorporated. Fill muffin tins to ⅔ full. Bake for 18–20 minutes. Cool slightly before serving.

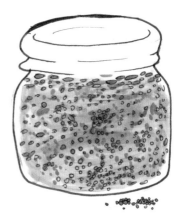

Gluten-Free Applesauce Doughnuts

If I were to assign a color to a season, I would have to choose gold for autumn. There is something so wonderful about the full, rich light that filters through the colored leaves of the trees. I love warm afternoons and dewy mornings in early autumn. As I move through autumn, I begin to feel pleasantly resigned to leaving the summer days behind and moving into the darkness of winter. Cozy evenings and crisp mornings become attractive.

One of the best parts of autumn is a trip to an apple orchard or a pumpkin patch. I love it when we manage to take an autumn afternoon to find our jack-o'-lantern pumpkins and pick fresh, crisp apples. It is so fun to watch littles pick apples! We have some darling pictures of our very small kiddos with huge apples that they can barely hold in their small hands, and I treasure them!

One highlight from these orchard excursions is the doughnut shack! The cakey applesauce doughnuts are a special treat. I love the smell of freshly cooked doughnuts, their cinnamon-sugared outsides, and the way the thin crisp exterior gives way to a pillowy center flecked with warm spices. Yum! This was one treat I wanted to be able to replicate post–celiac diagnosis, but it took me a while to accumulate the courage I needed to fry doughnuts. They turned out to be quite easy and not that messy. Try them and stop feeling left out when everyone else has doughnuts!

1 egg ¼ cup oil 1 cup applesauce ½ cup sugar 1 teaspoon vanilla	Whisk together in a large bowl.
2½ cups/354 grams gluten-free 　flour blend 1 teaspoon xanthan gum 1 teaspoon salt 2 teaspoons baking powder 1 teaspoon pumpkin pie spice blend *or* 　cinnamon Butter or nonstick cooking spray	Whisk dry ingredients lightly together, then thoroughly mix into the liquid ingredients. The resulting dough should be soft. Grease a 12x18-inch waxed muslin cloth or plastic wrap. Turn out the dough onto the cloth or wrap, then roll it into a rectangle ½-inch thick with a greased rolling pin. Cut doughnuts and holes with a doughnut cutter, or a large and a small cookie cutter.
4–5 cups peanut oil	Pour the oil into a large stockpot or flat-bottom carbon-steel wok (my preference) and heat the oil to 360 degrees F. Place raw doughnuts into the hot oil, 3–4 at a time, depending on the size of your pan. Cook doughnuts for about 2 minutes per side. Remove the doughnuts to drain for a few seconds on paper towels.
1 cup granulated sugar 1 tablespoon cinnamon	Mix together. While the doughnuts are still hot, roll them liberally in the cinnamon-sugar mixture. Remove doughnuts to a cooling rack to cool for a minute. Enjoy while they are still warm.

Flatbread

Flatbreads, such as this one, are one of the most ancient types of bread, baked on a hot surface rather than in an oven. I can easily imagine them as part of a subsistence lifestyle. Cooking over fires or on hot stones comes to mind. Hearty and forgiving, flatbread is a wonderful place for a novice to begin learning about yeasted breads. This recipe comes together pretty quickly and is satisfactorily crunchy at the edges and softer in the center. This bread makes a great accompaniment to just about anything, but it is especially suited to saucy stews and bean dishes that need a bit of sopping up at the end.

3 cups/425 grams all-purpose flour 1 cup/142 grams whole wheat flour 2 teaspoons salt	Whisk together in a large bowl.
1 teaspoon yeast 1 cup warm water 2 tablespoons honey ½ cup oil 1 egg, beaten	Whisk together. Stir the wet ingredients into the dry ingredients to form a rough dough. Knead for approximately 3–5 minutes to bring the dough together, then cover the bowl and rest the dough for 20 minutes.
	Preheat a frying pan or grill over medium heat. Turn out the dough onto a lightly floured surface. Cut the dough into four equal pieces and then cut each quarter into quarters. Roll out each quarter of dough into a ⅛-inch-thick bread. Place the dough on the hot pan and cook it until it gets puffy. Turn the bread and cook the other side. Cover the cooked bread to keep it warm.

Gluten-Free Variation: Whisk together 1½ teaspoons **yeast**, ¼ cup warm **water**, and 1 teaspoon **sugar**. Combine 2½ cups/354 grams **gluten-free flour blend**, ½ cup/60 grams **tapioca starch**, 1 cup/138 grams **garbanzo bean flour**, 1 teaspoon **salt**, and 1 tablespoon **xanthan gum** in a large bowl. When yeast mixture is foamy, stir it into the flour blend. Whisk together 1 cup warm **water**, ½ cup **oil**, 2 tablespoons **honey**, and 1 **egg**. Beat the egg mixture into the flour mixture until the dough is smooth. Preheat a griddle or a nonstick frying pan to 350 degrees F over medium heat. Flour your work surface and hands with **gluten-free flour**. Take a ¼- to ½-cup portion of dough and lightly form it into a ball. Start with smaller sizes and work towards larger sizes as you learn to work with this dough. Flatten the ball using a floured rolling pin on your floured work surface as thinly as possible without tearing the dough. Use a bench scraper or metal spatula to remove the dough from the rolling surface and place the dough on the heated griddle. Cook until the dough bubbles up. Check the bottom to make sure it is not burning. Flip the bread and finish cooking on the reverse side. Remove from the griddle and cover to keep warm. Repeat with the remaining dough. Freeze leftover flatbread to use the next time you have soup.

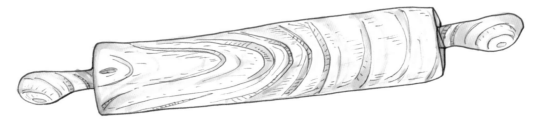

Dinner or Cinnamon Rolls

When I was growing up, my Aunt Juliann's rolls were a thing of legend—and quantity! She made pans and pans of them for family gatherings like birthdays, Christmas, and Thanksgiving. We all looked forward to them. I have no doubt that I ate more rolls than anything else at those dinners.

Aunt Juliann worked at a hospital near her house, but she often got up early and made a pan of cinnamon rolls before leaving for work. She made half of the pan with raisins and half without. When I was little, I was an ardent raisin-hater;

however, once, when only raisin cinnamon rolls were left, I tried one and discovered the lovely, plump sweetness that is cinnamon-sugar syruped raisins. Regardless of where you fall with respect to raisins, I suspect that you probably have a soft spot for cinnamon rolls. These are good!

Do let the dough rise in the refrigerator if you have time. Not only will the rolls be better, but the dough will be much easier to handle if it is cold. The dough for these rolls is and should be very wet.

Prep Time: 15 minutes • ***Rise Time:*** 5–8 hours • ***Cook Time:*** 20 minutes • ***Servings:*** 4–6

Roll Dough ¼ cup butter 2 cups hot milk 2 tablespoons oil ⅓ cup honey 2 eggs, lightly beaten	Cut the butter into pieces and stir into the hot milk. Add the oil and honey once the butter melts. Whisk the eggs into the milk mixture.
4 cups/480 grams all-purpose flour 1 cup whole wheat flour 1½ teaspoons salt 2 teaspoons yeast	Whisk together in a large bowl or a stand mixer bowl. Gradually stir in the milk mixture. Continue to stir and fold for five minutes. Cover the bowl with plastic wrap and refrigerate for 5–8 hours.
½ cup flour, divided Butter or nonstick cooking spray ¼ cup butter, melted	Sprinkle 1/4 cup flour on your work surface. Turn the dough out onto the flour. Sprinkle another 1/4 cup of flour on top of the dough. Roll the dough out until it is approximately ½ inch thick. Grease a half-sheet baking pan. Use a biscuit cutter to cut circles of dough. Brush a bit of butter on the center of the dough, and fold each circle over so that the top is slightly smaller than the bottom. Arrange the rolls on the pan with the rolls touching. Once all the rolls are cut and folded, brush the tops with the remaining butter. Allow the rolls to rise, uncovered, for 20 minutes. Five minutes into the rise, preheat the oven to 350 degrees F. Bake for 18–20 minutes. Enjoy warm. >

Dinner or Cinnamon Rolls

For cinnamon rolls

½ cup butter

⅓ cup white sugar

¼ cup brown sugar

2 tablespoons cornstarch

2 tablespoons cinnamon

2 teaspoons honey

⅔ cup raisins (optional)

Icing

¼ cup very soft butter

⅓ cup Greek yogurt

2 cups/240 grams powdered sugar

1 teaspoon vanilla

1 pinch salt

Grease a 9x13-inch pan. Follow the directions above for turning out the dough with the flour. Flatten the dough into a ½-inch-thick rectangle. Combine butter, sugars, cornstarch, and cinnamon. Spread evenly over dough. Drizzle honey over the filling. Sprinkle the raisins evenly over the dough, if desired. Roll the long edge along itself. You may need to use a floured bench scraper to help with the rolling. Using the bench scraper, cut the log of dough in half, cut each half in half, then each half into thirds, for a total of 12 rolls. Place in prepared pan. Allow the rolls to rise, uncovered, for 1 hour. 45 minutes into the rise, preheat the oven to 350 degrees F. Bake rolls for 20–23 minutes or until just golden. Beat together icing ingredients until fluffy. Allow rolls to cool, then spread icing over them.

🌾 *Gluten-Free Variation:* Combine 2 tablespoons warm **water**, 1½ teaspoons **yeast**, and ½ teaspoon **sugar** in a small bowl. Combine 1 cup/142 grams **gluten-free flour blend**, ¾ cup/85 grams **tapioca flour**, and 1 cup/69 grams **garbanzo bean flour**, 2½ teaspoons **xanthan gum**, and ¾ teaspoon **salt** in a large mixing bowl (use a stand mixer if you have one—this recipe involves a lot of beating). Whisk together in a medium bowl ⅔ cup warm **water**, 2 tablespoons + 2 teaspoons **oil**, and ¼ cup **sugar**. Pour the water mixture into the flour mixture and beat to combine. When the yeast is foamy, add it to the mixture as well, scrape the sides, and mix again. Beat in 2 **eggs**, one at a time, scraping the bottom of the bowl after each addition. Using a stand mixer with the dough hook attachment (ideally), beat the dough for 8 minutes, scrape the sides, and beat for an additional 5 minutes. Allow the dough to rest for 20 minutes. Line a rimmed half-sheet pan with parchment, or grease with nonstick cooking spray.

For dinner rolls: Flour your work surface with **gluten-free flour**. Have a bench scraper and rolling pin at hand. Turn the dough out on the surface and lightly flour the top. Gently roll the dough to a thickness of ½ inch. Use a lightly floured round cookie cutter to cut circles in the dough. Use the bench scraper to remove the dough from the work surface if necessary. Lightly flour your hands and gently pat the edges of the rolls toward the center of the roll to tidy up the edges. Place the rolls 1 inch apart on the parchment-lined baking sheet. Cover the baking sheet with a second rimmed half-sheet pan and allow the rolls to rise for 45–60 minutes, or until they have doubled in size. Preheat the oven to 325 degrees F and bake for 25–30 minutes or until the rolls are golden and interior temperature registers 200 degrees F.

For cinnamon rolls: Soften ¼ cup **butter**. Preheat the oven to 325 degrees F. Generously grease a 9x13-inch baking dish. Liberally flour your work surface with **gluten-free flour** and turn half of the dough out onto this surface. Flour the top of the dough as needed and keep a bench scraper or metal spatula handy in case the dough sticks to your surface. Flatten the dough into a large ¼-inch-thick rectangle. Gently spread the very soft butter evenly over this surface. Combine 3 tablespoons **granulated sugar**, 2 tablespoons **brown sugar**, 1½ teaspoons **cornstarch**, and 1 tablespoon **cinnamon**. Sprinkle half of this mixture over the butter. Add **raisins** if desired. Drizzle approximately 2 teaspoons **honey** over the sugar mixture. Carefully roll the dough, using the bench scraper if it sticks, and seal the end by gently pinching it into the rest of the roll. Cut the log into 1-inch sections and use the bench scraper to transfer these to the prepared baking dish. Repeat with the second half of the dough. Cover and allow the rolls to rise for 45–60 minutes, or until they have doubled in bulk. Bake the rolls for 25–30 minutes until the tops are golden. Allow the rolls to cool if you want the frosting to not melt.

Icing: See icing recipe on page 130.

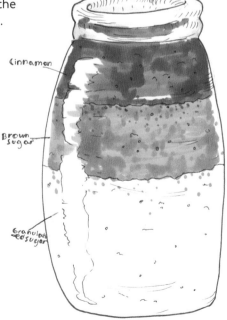

Cinnamon

Brown sugar

Granulated sugar

Gluten-Free Baguette

Mom and Dad took me and Kleine to many different restaurants when we were growing up, and I was always curious about the rolls or breads that would be served when we were seated at the table. I often could have made a meal of the bread and butter alone! Some of my favorite rolls and breads were like a baguette, with a crisp crust and a nicely springy interior. There really is not much that beats such bread for sopping up sauce or adorning with butter.

I missed this bread after my celiac diagnosis. In talking to friends who have made similar dietary transitions, I have found that the experience of mourning over breads and baked goods is pretty common. It's easy to feel out of it when attending group dinners and potlucks where the comestibles have the potential to hugely disrupt your life for a month. This might sound melodramatic for those who have not witnessed or experienced a bad reaction to gluten, but it is unfortunately true. So—what to do? Figure out a new recipe, of course! This gluten-free baguette has received rave reviews from gluten-free and conventional eaters alike. While the crust isn't as crisp as a wheat flour–based baguette (we owe that crispiness to the gluten coat that develops in the folding process), the interior of the baguette is nicely springy and beautifully textured. In my house, this loaf is highly anticipated by conventional and gluten-free eaters alike.

2 tablespoons warm water 1 teaspoon sugar 2 teaspoons yeast	Whisk together in a small bowl and allow to sit until foamy.
¾ cup/105 grams gluten-free flour blend ½ cup/70 grams tapioca starch ½ cup/70 grams garbanzo bean flour 1½ teaspoons xanthan gum ¾ teaspoon salt 1 tablespoon sugar	Whisk together in a large bowl to combine.
¾ cup warm water 1 tablespoon olive oil	Whisk together and stir into the flour mixture. Stir yeast mixture into the flour mixture. Using a stand mixer with a dough hook attachment (ideally), beat the mixture for 5–7 minutes until the dough is homogeneous and the beater leaves a clear track through the dough. It will not gather around the beater like a gluten dough. Allow the dough to rest for 20 minutes.
Parchment paper Small bowl of water Bench scraper	Generously flour your work surface. Turn the dough onto the work surface. Dampen your hands with water and flatten the dough into a rectangle. Use the bench scraper to fold the dough over onto itself in thirds. Gently roll the dough into a 12–15 inch loaf. Use damp hands to smooth the top of the dough. Roll the dough onto the parchment and place the parchment on a baking sheet. Slash the dough top in three places. Allow the dough to rise, covered, for 45–60 minutes, or until it has doubled in size. During the final 20 minutes of rising, preheat the oven to 400 degrees F. Bake the risen dough for 25–30 minutes. Cool at least 25–30 minutes before slicing.

BAKING AND CANDY

Pastry

Pie—specifically fruit pie—seemed to be everywhere when I was a little girl, which was a shame because I was not really a fan of it. I loved the sugar-crusted top and the crispy crimped edge of crust *around* the pie. Even some of the gooey juice along the edges of the crust had a little merit. The problem with pie, as far as my young palate was concerned, was the squishy cooked fruit. I had yet to appreciate fruit in cooked form. Then, one sunny summer day when I was really hungry after an afternoon swim, I tried my Aunt Gretchen's peach pie. The peaches were sunny and not noticeably squishy, although they were wonderfully tender, and the sweet juice mingled enticingly with the crumbly crust. I decided that I liked pie after all, and I have never looked back, which just goes to show that sometimes we just need to be a little patient with the evolution of our children's palates!

The following pie pastry is a good foundation for any fruit or savory pie, and the cobbler recipe is the perfect dessert for a busy day when you need a low-maintenance fruit dessert. I hope you enjoy the pie.

Cakes and Cookies

I love cake. I love the creamy sweetness of frosting as a counterpoint to the airy richness of the cake itself. I love the absolute decadence of butter and egg and sugar. Good cake invites you to have a second slice even if you know better. Really good cake does not require the companionship of ice cream, so theoretically you could enjoy that second slice without too much guilt! Whether simply decorated with pink icing and candles or decadently stuffed with candies and drizzled with ganache and caramel, cake is almost always a project that I look forward to.

Fresh cookies, on the other hand, are simple pleasures from the point at which sugar and butter are first creamed together. Since they are quick to make, cookies can be a great way to add a little sweetness to your loved ones' days. I always loved that Mom almost always slipped a couple of chocolate chip cookies into my lunch box when I was in school—along with notes of encouragement.

Cakes and cookies fall squarely into the indulgence category, and as such they are a great way to show a little extra love to the people you care about. Here are a few favorite recipes that I make over and over again for the people I love.

Baked Treats

45 Minutes to 3 Hours

Pie Pastry

There's something incredibly comforting about pie, evocative of togetherness and a probably idealized memory of how good things were when we were young. In those moments our biggest troubles were easily soothed away with some time by our parents' sides and a little taste of their food. I realize that not everyone has this kind of memory. But regardless of how we grew up, we can and should always create this security for our children. This security can come as we make pie together, watch it bake, impatiently wait for it to cool, and eat it together.

About a year after my celiac diagnosis, I began feeling very nostalgic for pie, probably because I had been reading *Farmer Boy* by Laura Ingalls Wilder to Bear. The pie is always described so tantalizingly in that book—flaky golden crust, spiced

sweet juice, etc. I enjoyed the descriptions but resigned myself to life without pie since gluten-free pie pastry was difficult to produce with any success. It was sad, but there's more to life than pie . . .

Then I had a revelatory visit to Origins Bakery in Victoria, British Columbia. I learned about binding pie crust with cream cheese and once again tasted a crumbly crust against that lovely pie juice. When I made my first crust, I felt like I'd accomplished something quite grand! When a gluten-eating friend tasted it and pronounced it "beautiful," I really felt like I'd gotten somewhere. The pastry made with wheat flour and the one made with gluten-free flour are both lovely pie crusts.

2 cups/283 grams all-purpose flour 1 cup/142 grams whole wheat flour 1 teaspoon salt 2 tablespoons sugar	Whisk together in a large bowl to combine.
½ cup/96 grams cold shortening ½ cup cold butter	Add the shortening and butter to the flour mixture and toss to coat. Rub the fat into the flour with your hands until it looks uniformly crumbly. The flour mixture should pack and fall apart like damp sand.
1 cup cold water 3 ice cubes 1 teaspoon distilled white vinegar	Combine ingredients in a small bowl. Drizzle ½ cup water evenly over the flour mixture to start. Quickly press the water into the flour. Make sure to bring any residual dry mixture up from the bottom. Add additional tablespoons of water and continue to press it into the flour until the dough is uniformly moistened and no dry spots remain.
	Divide the dough into two parts. Flatten each into a five-inch diameter disk and wrap with plastic wrap. Chill or freeze for at least 20 minutes before rolling out to hold your favorite pie filling.

Gluten-Free Variation: You will need a pizza peel or a flat, unrimmed baking sheet for this recipe. Combine in a large bowl 2½ cups/312 grams **gluten-free flour blend**, ½ teaspoon **xanthan gum**, and ½ teaspoon **salt**. Cut 12 tablespoons cold salted **butter** into ¼-inch cubes. Scatter cubes over the flour mixture. Rub butter into flour with your fingers until the mixture looks evenly damp and no large pieces remain. Fold ½ cup **Greek yogurt** into the flour mixture until the mixture is homogeneous. You cannot overwork this dough. Divide the dough into two equal portions. Generously flour the baking sheet or peel with **potato starch**, **tapioca starch**, or **cornstarch**. Roll the dough to ⅛-inch thickness. Use the dough scraper to loosen the edges and make sure the middle is not stuck. Gently shake the pastry dough into the pie dish. Repair any cracks as necessary by patching in pie dough scraps. For a single-crust pie, crimp the edges and prick the dough with a fork, then blind-bake at 400 degrees F until golden and crisp. For a two-crust pie, add your choice of filling, cover with the second crust, and bake at 400 degrees F until golden and crisp (and bubbly if you are baking a fruit pie).

Berry Cobbler

I often get carried away with U-pick produce. The whole experience of picking produce at U-pick farms is satisfactory to me: I know I'm supporting small farms and small businesses; I am outside in the sunshine and enjoying the fruits of an expert's labors; I love the feel of the fruit or vegetables in my hands. I even like the dirt! The upshot of all of this is that it's not uncommon for me to come home with more produce than I am realistically going to be able to freeze or can or just eat before it goes bad. When I'm faced with this challenge, I know it's time to bake.

Somewhere between a cake and a pie, cobbler is a quick option for a lovely dessert if you are too busy for pie and have a lot of fruit on your hands. My favorite fruits for cobbler are berries, but many other fruits work just as well. A topping of ice cream produces a dessert that is pure summer perfection—sweet, creamy, and casual.

Butter or nonstick cooking spray 2 pounds fresh or frozen berries and/or cherries 1 cup sugar 2 tablespoons cornstarch 1 lemon, zested and juiced	Grease a 3-quart baking dish and preheat the oven to 350 degrees F. Toss the berries with the sugar, cornstarch, lemon juice, and zest. Add the berry mixture to the baking dish.
2 cups/284 grams all-purpose flour 1 tablespoon baking powder ½ teaspoon salt 1 cup sugar	Whisk together.
½ cup cold butter, cubed ¼ cup milk ½ cup yogurt 2 eggs 1 teaspoon vanilla	Cut cold butter into the flour mixture with a pastry blender, or rub it in with your fingers. Whisk together milk, yogurt, eggs, and vanilla and fold this into the flour mixture until everything is evenly moist. Spoon globs of this dough evenly over the top of the fruit.
1 tablespoon sugar Vanilla ice cream	Sprinkle pastry with sugar. Place the cobbler in the center of the preheated oven and bake for 1 hour and 15 minutes. Check to see if the cobbler is baked through. Cool slightly before serving with ice cream.

Gluten-Free Variation: Follow the instructions as directed above, except use 2 cups/284 grams **gluten-free flour blend** and ¾ teaspoon **xanthan gum** instead of the all-purpose **flour**.

Chocolate Angel Food Cake

Mimi always made "The Cake" for Papa's birthday in mid-April, and she often decorated it with the pansies that had begun popping out of the spring-damp earth on the farm where they lived. Kleine and I loved picking pansies for the cake. Mimi had a huge yard, and she loved her flowers. She let the pansies grow wherever they sprang up. There were hundreds from spring until frost: purple with yellow hearts, light purple with dark purple hearts, dark purple with black hearts. I never could decide what kind I liked best. Pansies are edible and do make a lovely garnish to the chocolate angel food cake if you happen to have a few in your yard, and they haven't been treated with herbicides or pesticides.

I asked Mimi to teach me how to make this cake when I was in high school. I joined her in her little yellow kitchen one afternoon, and she got out her old church community cookbook with the red cover. She did not use a stand mixer, so making an angel cake meant beating egg whites by hand. It was a good workout! Chocolate angel food cake is simultaneously rich and airy. It is wonderful. Perhaps it can become a family tradition for you too!

¾ cup sifted cake flour

¾ cup + 2 tablespoons superfine sugar

¼ cup cocoa powder

Preheat oven to 350 degrees F. Wash and dry your tube pan or angel food cake pan to ensure that it is completely free of any oil. Measure flour by sifting it into measuring cups and then leveling it off with the straight side of a knife. Sift the flour, sugar, and cocoa together three times and set aside.

1½ cups cold egg whites (this may take a full dozen eggs)

1½ teaspoons cream of tartar

¼ teaspoon salt

1½ teaspoons vanilla

¾ cup superfine sugar

Beat egg whites, cream of tartar, salt, and vanilla until foamy. Increase the mixer speed to medium-high. Gradually trickle the sugar into the egg whites while beating them. Continue beating until stiff glossy peaks form.

Sprinkle 3 tablespoons of the flour mixture over the beaten egg whites and fold together with a large, clean spatula. Avoid stirring! Lift up some batter and then draw the spatula edge through the foam. Repeat with remaining flour. Spoon the batter into the pan and spread it smooth on top. Cut through the batter with a knife to remove any air pockets. Bake the cake for 50–60 minutes, or until top of cake springs back when touched lightly. Do not check the cake before 50 minutes have lapsed. Invert cake in pan to cool. >

Chocolate Angel Food Cake

⅓ cup Dutch-process or Special Dark cocoa

¾ cup sugar

2 cups cold whipping cream

While the cake is baking and cooling, whisk these ingredients thoroughly, but do not beat the mixture. Refrigerate. Once the cake is cool, cut around the outside and inside edges to loosen the cake. Remove it from the pan and cut into three equal layers with a serrated knife.

Beat the cream mixture until stiff. Spread approximately 1 cup of whipped cream between each layer and spread the remainder on the outside of the cake. Decorative whorls are fun to make with the back of the spoon in the cream. Decorate with edible flowers if desired. It's best eaten on the same day it is made.

🌾 *Gluten-Free Variation:* If you are using volumetric measurements here instead of weights, spoon the flour into the cup and then level off with a knife. Instead of cake flour, combine in the pitcher of a high-speed blender 2 tablespoons/24 grams **sorghum flour**, 2 tablespoons/28 grams **sweet rice flour**, ¾ cup plus 2 tablespoons **granulated sugar**. Blend on high for two minutes. Add ¼ cup/32 grams **tapioca starch**, and ¾ teaspoon **xanthan gum**. Use this mixture instead of the cake flour in the recipe.

Tip: This cake is a bit finicky because it's leavened only with egg whites. The first time I helped Mimi make this, I'd separated all of the egg whites perfectly—and then I broke the yolk on the last one. That yolk spoiled the whole batch, and we had to start over. Mimi was very patient; I definitely learned my lesson to be careful. The egg whites should be from the freshest eggs you can find. Fresh egg whites hold their structure better than old. It's also critical to keep them free of any fat. When separating them, pour each into a little cup as you are separating it, then add it to the measuring cup with the rest. Take care to sift the flour and cocoa three times, as directed. This is essential for a fluffy cake fit for angels! If you take a little care, you will be rewarded with a lovely cake.

Shelf Life

This table is not meant to be a definitive guide to everything, but it will provide you with some conservative parameters for storing perishables. For prepared perishables, such as leftover commercially prepared chicken stock, pay attention to the storage guidelines on the packaging. Always use your nose to determine if the item in question smells spoiled. Marking the date on refrigerated or frozen items before putting them in the refrigerator or freezer is crucial, so keep a permanent marker handy in the kitchen. Finally, if you don't have an immediate use for leftovers, try to break them down. For instance, bone and shred leftover chicken, and put it in a labeled container in the freezer immediately. This helps to avoid wasted leftovers. Do not throw away bones! You can always use them to make stock. Keep a container in the freezer that you can add to, then make stock when you have enough bones.

Perishable	Conservative Refrigerator Life
Raw meats and poultry	2–3 days or pull date. (You can freeze meats to be used later.)
Seafood	Flash frozen seafood is the freshest. Remove plastic packaging, thaw in the refrigerator, and use the same day. Use thawed seafood on the day it is purchased.
Cooked meats/casseroles	4–5 days (freeze immediately if you won't use it within this time).
Homemade stocks and soups	2–3 days (freeze immediately if you won't use it within this time).
Hard cheeses	Trim any mold off the cheese prior to use.
Soft cheeses	5–6 days after opening.
Yogurt/buttermilk	7–21 days after opening.
Butter	Up to one month; frozen up to 6 months.
Leafy greens	6–7 days (vitamin content declines with time, so use close to purchase date).
Root vegetables/hard fruits	2–3 weeks.
Mayonnaise and related condiments	1 month to several months.

Almond Texas Sheet Cake

When Hervor was born we invited quite a few family members to come to her baby blessing at church and then to our house afterward for lunch. We had this simple cake for dessert, and everyone loved it so much that I decided to try to enter it in the Pillsbury Bake-Off. It didn't get selected, but we still love it anyway. The crunchy, sweet toffee and roasted almonds are the perfect counterpoint to the buttery cake.

Sheet cakes such as this one seem to have impossible ingredient proportions, but they work in a way that is quick and magical. This is a wonderful dessert option if I find myself pressed for time before an event to which I said I would bring a dessert. Who am I kidding—I'm always pressed for time! Maybe that is why I like this cake so much. You even have to frost the cake while it is still warm, so it's possible to get from ingredients to finished cake in less than an hour, which is perfect when I have crammed more into my day than the hours will allow.

Butter or nonstick cooking spray 3 cups/425 grams flour 2 cups sugar 1½ teaspoons baking powder ½ teaspoon salt	Preheat oven to 350 degrees F. Grease a rimmed half-sheet pan. Whisk together the dry ingredients.
1 cup butter ¾ cup water	Combine in saucepan and stir the mixture frequently while it comes to a boil. When stirring does not remove the bubbles (a rolling boil), remove the pan from the heat.
2 eggs ½ cup plain yogurt 1½ teaspoons vanilla 1 teaspoon almond extract	Beat together until thoroughly combined. Whisk these into the butter mixture, then stir in the flour mixture, and mix until the batter is mostly smooth. Pour the batter into the prepared baking sheet and place it in the oven. Bake for 20–25 minutes.
Icing ¾ cup butter ¼ cup milk 4½ cups/482 grams powdered sugar 1 teaspoon vanilla ½ teaspoon almond extract 1 pinch salt 1 cup toffee bits 1 cup toasted almond slivers	For the browned butter icing, cook the butter over medium heat until it foams and then turns light brown. Remove immediately from the heat and beat in the milk and powdered sugar. Mix in the extracts and salt. Pour the warm icing over the warm cake. Sprinkle warm frosting with toasted almonds and toffee bits.

Gluten-Free Variation: Use 3 cups/425 grams **gluten-free flour blend** and 1 teaspoon **xanthan gum** instead of the all-purpose **flour** in the recipe.

Brownies

When I was growing up, Mom routinely baked her chocolate chip cookies like brownies in a 9x13-inch baking dish. These chocolate chip bars were so good. They must have satisfied my family's desire for gooey chocolatiness, because I never really enjoyed brownies much until I graduated from high school and went off to college. At college, I was introduced to a brownie with mint frosting and chocolate ganache, and I also had friends who loved brownies so much that they ate the dry mix from the box, so my opinion about brownies began to change. I started to appreciate the plain brownie, the caramel brownie, the peanut-butter-cup brownie, and so on. Brownies entered the desserts-worthy-of-consumption list. Unfortunately, even among the great brownies, there were also many brownies that were dry and flat tasting. I found that I had grown into a picky eater when it came to brownies.

After celiac I developed quite a few baking recipes before I got to brownies. The initial results were discouragingly dry and boring, and it took some persistence to find a formula for the basic ingredients that was just right. Whether baked with wheat flour or gluten-free flours, these brownies have the requisite shattering crust, crisp edges, and chocolatey interior that will satisfy the fudgy brownie enthusiast.

Butter or nonstick cooking spray 1 cup sugar ¼ cup brown sugar 1 cup/142 grams all-purpose flour ½ cup/42 grams cocoa powder ½ teaspoon baking powder ¼ teaspoon salt 1 cup chocolate chips	Preheat oven to 350 degrees F. Grease an 8-inch-square baking dish. Combine all ingredients in a medium bowl.
2 eggs ½ cup soft butter 1 teaspoon vanilla	Beat eggs, butter, and vanilla together. Stir flour mixture into the butter mixture until the flour is evenly moistened and no dry streaks remain. Pour the batter into the prepared baking dish and bake for 25–30 minutes, or until the middle is just set and the edges are crisp.

Gluten-Free Variation: Use 1 cup/142 grams **gluten-free flour blend** and ½ teaspoon **xanthan gum** instead of the all-purpose **flour**. Bake for 35–40 minutes.

Peanut Butter Chocolate Chip Cookies

When Hervor, Bear, and Nancy D were small we read books every day. Without a heavy schedule, we had time to just read and snuggle. After lunch we had storytime on the couch. I would get a great stack of books and set out happily to read through them. I often fell asleep mid-story, particularly if sleeping the night before had been interrupted by three little kiddos. Despite impromptu naps, we spent hours reading.

One of Hervor's favorite series was Arnold Lobel's Frog and Toad. We loved that the effervescent Frog was the perfect foil for the pessimistic Toad, and enjoyed the side characters like the birds and the snail. Hervor loved them enough to request a Frog and Toad party for her fourth birthday. I made these cookies to represent the irresistible cookies from the story "Cookies" in *Frog and Toad Together*.

They're also the base for a gluten-free family treat we call s'moreos. Nancy D coined the name when we made s'mores with two peanut butter chocolate chip cookies instead of graham crackers. The s'moreos were delicious. Cookies crisp on the edges and soft in the middle, studded with melted chocolate, which is how I wish my chocolate in the s'more would be anyway! The s'moreo was an instant summer classic for our family. We enjoy it when we have a fire in our backyard fire pit.

1 cup/142 grams all-purpose flour 1 cup/142 grams whole wheat flour 1 teaspoon baking powder 1 teaspoon salt	Preheat the oven to 350 degrees F. Whisk together.
1 cup butter, slightly softened ⅔ cup brown sugar ¾ cup granulated sugar 2 tablespoons honey	Beat the butter until it is creamy then beat in the sugars and honey. Continue to beat until the mixture is light and creamy.
2 eggs 1 teaspoon vanilla extract 1 cup smooth peanut butter (such as Jif)	Add eggs one at a time, scraping the bowl after each egg is incorporated, and then the vanilla and peanut butter. Beat this mixture until smooth. Reduce the speed to low and gradually stir in the flour mixture.
1 cup chocolate chips 1½ cups peanut butter chips	Stir the chips into the dough. Drop tablespoon-sized dough balls onto a baking sheet. Bake 10 minutes. Allow cookies to cool one minute on baking sheet and then remove them to cooling racks.
Peanut butter filling 1 cup/250 grams smooth peanut butter ½ cup butter, softened 1½ cups powdered sugar 2 tablespoons honey 1 teaspoon salt	Beat these ingredients together until smooth. Spread on the flat side of one cooled cookie, then add another cooled cookie to the top to make a sandwich. Continue with the rest of the cookies. You can also use toasted marshmallows as the sandwich filling. Enjoy!

Gluten-Free Variation: Preheat the oven to 350 degrees F. In a medium bowl, combine 1½ cups/211 grams **gluten-free flour blend**, ½ teaspoon **baking powder**, ½ teaspoon **salt**, ½ teaspoon **xanthan gum**. To a large mixing bowl, add ½ cup softened **butter**, 2 tablespoons oil, ⅔ cup **brown sugar**, ⅔ cup **granulated sugar**, and 1 tablespoon **honey**. Beat together for a couple of minutes until the mixture is light and fluffy. Beat 1 **egg** into the sugar mixture and scrape the sides and beat again. Beat in 1 teaspoon **vanilla** and ½ cup/125 grams **smooth peanut butter** until the mixture is smooth. Reduce the mixer speed to low and mix in the **flour blend** until it is thoroughly combined. Stir in 1 cup **chocolate chips** and 1 cup **peanut butter chips**. Drop tablespoon-sized dough balls onto a greased or parchment-lined baking sheet. Bake the cookies for 11–13 minutes, or until the tops are set and the edges are turning golden. Allow the cookies to sit on the baking sheet for about 30 seconds before removing them to cooling racks to cool completely. Sandwich with the peanut butter filling in the recipe above or with **toasted marshmallows** as desired.

Cutout Sugar Cookies

I can't imagine a holiday, particularly Halloween or Valentine's Day, without cutout sugar cookies. When Mom got out the Halloween cookie cutters and said it was time to make sugar cookies, Kleine and I would get excited, but it felt like the dough-chilling portion took forever! Two whole hours! You will still need to chill the dough if you are making these cookies with all-purpose flour, but if you are making the gluten-free variation, you should roll and cut the cookies immediately.

All my kiddos—but especially Nancy D and Dr. Lu—like helping with the cutting and decorating of these sugar cookies.

These cookies are good both when the dough is rolled thickly then cooked until they are set but not crisp, as well as when they're rolled thin and cooked until they are golden brown. Choose your preferred style or try both to find your favorite.

Prep Time: 15 minutes · *Chill Time:* 1–2 hours · *Cook Time:* 30 minutes · *Servings:* varies

3½ cups/496 grams all-purpose flour 1 teaspoon baking powder ½ teaspoon salt	Whisk together.
1 cup butter, softened 1 cup sugar ½ cup/60 grams powdered sugar	Beat the butter until it is creamy and beat in the sugars. Continue to beat until the mixture is thoroughly blended.
1½ teaspoons vanilla 2 eggs	Beat vanilla and eggs into sugar mixture. Scrape sides of the bowl and continue to beat until the mixture becomes fluffy. Reduce mixer speed to low and beat in the flour. Continue to beat until the flour is completely incorporated. Form the dough into two 1-inch-thick discs, wrap in plastic wrap, and chill for an hour or two. Roll out the dough to your desired thickness. Using cookie cutters, cut the dough into desired shapes and arrange on parchment-lined baking sheets. Sprinkle with granulated sugar if you do not want to make the lemon glaze below. Preheat the oven to 350 degrees F and bake for 8–10 minutes or until just beginning to turn golden brown. Remove to racks to cool.
Icing 4 cups/480 grams powdered sugar ¼ cup light corn syrup ⅓ cup milk 1 teaspoon vanilla 1 pinch salt 1 tablespoon + 1 teaspoon lemon juice Food coloring, as desired Sprinkles or decorating sugars, as desired	Whisk powdered sugar, corn syrup, milk, vanilla, salt, and lemon juice together until smooth. Tint as desired. Drizzle on cookies or dip cookies in icing. Decorate with decorative sugars or sprinkles as desired.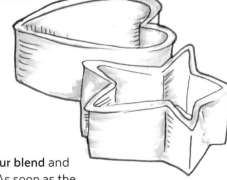

Gluten-Free Variation: Use 3½ cups/496 grams **gluten-free flour blend** and 1½ teaspoons **xanthan gum** instead of the regular all-purpose flour. As soon as the dough is mixed, generously flour your work surface and roll the dough out to your desired thickness. Cut cookies and place on parchment-lined baking sheets. Sprinkle with **sugar** if you are not going to make the lemon glaze. Bake for 10–13 minutes at 350 degrees F.

There is something magical in how sugar and butter mingle and caramelize and transform into the crumbly, rich stuff that is candy. There is a nostalgic magic in my memory when I think of making homemade candy with Grandma-Great in her kitchen, which, more often than not, smelled of butter and sugar and chocolate. When I was in fourth grade, Grandma began teaching me the art of candy making. She first learned how to make honey taffy from her father and then honed her candy-making skills by taking classes every time she had a chance.

I remember standing by her stove as she explained why washing down the sides of a pan full of boiling sugar syrup with a pastry brush dipped in water could control the formation of sugar crystals in the finished candy. It was hot and a little scary, and I felt so grown up. I smelled all of her flavoring oils as we tried to decide which would be the best for the taffy we were going to be pulling. Taffy pulling is a great workout, and I was vastly impressed by my grandma's strong, capable arms and deft knife work. During those visits, I also loved poring over her candy cookbooks and supply catalogues and tantalizing myself with visions of making the gorgeous treats in the pictures—especially the pink divinity and homemade lollipops. For me, visits to Grandma-Great's house are synonymous with candy. Even when I visited her shortly before her passing at 98½ years old, I found a tin of her homemade candy waiting for visitors who stopped by. Maybe there is something magical about her candy after all.

Once you get the hang of candy, it is so much fun to make and eat—and homemade candy never fails to impress on special occasions. Make sure to read the instructions thoroughly before you begin. A candy thermometer and some kind of cooling surface (a marble slab is the best, but a cold cookie sheet will do) are really the only special equipment you need.

Homemade candy is always a welcome treat, and it travels much more successfully than cookies or cakes. It is a really good option if you want to send someone you love a care package. These candies are slightly more complicated than baked sweets, but as long as you pay attention and work quickly when you need to, they're not that hard to make. Remember to decrease the target cooking temperature 1 degree Fahrenheit for every 550-foot increase in elevation above sea level. So, where I live, at approximately 2,300 feet above sea level, I would cook candy that needed to get to 305 degrees F to approximately 301 degrees F.

Candy

3–6 Hours

English Toffee

If there's one candy that I associate with Christmastime, it's English toffee. As a little girl, I used to "help" Grandma-Great make it when she came to visit, or when we went to her house. Sometimes, she sent Mom big cans of it if we weren't going to see each other before Christmas. Then Mom, Kleine, and I would spend a Saturday afternoon frosting each individual piece with chocolate and chopped nuts before placing it on a piece of waxed paper to set. It was so hard to keep from licking my chocolatey nut-encrusted fingers during the frosting process—and sometimes I did give way to that temptation.

Everyone loves the English toffee. When I was little, it was an essential part of many Christmas gifts to neighbors and friends, and it was always one of the highlights of the Dinner Group Christmas Party cookie exchange. Because the toffee was so yummy, often there was no toffee left for the actual exchange because everyone had eaten it. Mom began bringing separate packages of toffee for everyone to take home afterwards. It is a treasure! You should try it. You might make new friends with it.

2 tablespoons vegetable oil	Drizzle on marble slab or large baking sheet. Use a paper towel or your clean hands to spread the oil evenly over the surface.
2 cups butter 2 tablespoons light corn syrup *or* Lyle's golden syrup ⅓ cup water 2½ cups sugar 1 teaspoon salt	Place ingredients in a large, heavy pot and bring to a boil over medium-low heat. Cook, stirring and scraping the sides and bottom periodically, until the syrup reaches 294 degrees F on a candy thermometer. Wash down the sides two or three times during the cooking process by running a pastry brush dipped in cold water along the sides of the pot.
2 cups roasted salted almonds, coarsely chopped into ⅛ to ¼-inch pieces	Stir the almonds into the syrup. Pour the syrup evenly out onto the prepared slab. Run a large knife under the candy to make sure it is not sticking. Score the candy by pressing a knife blade into the soft candy in 1½-inch-wide rows and then 1½-inch squares. Let cool completely, then break into individual pieces.
1 pound chocolate, chopped 2 cups roasted salted almonds, finely chopped	Lay out wax paper to put the toffee pieces on after dipping. Melt ⅔ of the chocolate in a double boiler or using your microwave's setting for melting chocolate. Stir until smooth and then stir in the remaining chocolate until completely melted. If it will not melt after a few minutes of stirring, heat very briefly and stir again. Cover toffee pieces on all sides with melted chocolate, then dip in the almonds. Place chocolate-and-almond covered pieces on waxed paper to set.

 *Gluten-Free Variation:* This recipe is naturally gluten-free.

Peanut Butter Brittle

One of the first regional treats I enjoyed when I met Mr. Kent's family for the first time was soft peanut brittle, a locally famous candy that is served at Spokane's most special hotel, the Davenport. Mr. Kent's family had a box from a friend the first time we spent Christmas with his family. It was so good—like the inside of a Butterfinger bar—but fresher and better. The flakiness of the candy took me by surprise because I was accustomed to the traditional hard peanut brittle that can actually break your teeth (or pull your fillings out). I decided right away that I needed to learn how to make this special candy. This is one of the more finicky recipes in the book with lots of coordination and last-minute actions. Make sure to read through the recipe all the way and get everything set out before you begin.

2 tablespoons vegetable oil	Drizzle on marble slab or large cooled baking sheet. Use a paper towel or your clean hands to spread the oil evenly over the surface.
2 cups smooth peanut butter 1 teaspoon baking soda 1 teaspoon water	Melt peanut butter in the microwave on the chocolate melting setting. Combine the baking soda and water and set aside for later.
¼ cup water 1½ cups corn syrup 1½ cups sugar ½ teaspoon salt	Combine ingredients in a large, heavy pot and place the pan over medium heat. Bring the mixture to a boil until it reaches 305 degrees F on a candy thermometer. Wash down the sides two or three times during the cooking process by running a pastry brush dipped in cold water along the sides of the pot.
2 cups roasted salted peanuts, coarsely chopped 2 tablespoons butter	When the candy reaches 305 degrees F, stir in peanuts and butter. The temperature of the candy will drop. Keep the candy on the heat while stirring very frequently to return the temperature to 290 degrees F without burning the peanuts.
Melted peanut butter Baking soda and water mixture	Quickly but thoroughly fold in the warm peanut butter. The candy will thicken noticeably. Stir in the baking soda and water mixture and expect the candy to foam up. Pour/scrape the candy onto the prepared slab using a utensil in each hand (i.e., a bench scraper and a large spoon) to spread the candy as thinly as possible. It will clump up a bit and break apart a little—this is okay. Score the candy using a large knife into 1½-inch-wide rows and then 1½-inch squares. Cool completely, then break into pieces. Store in an airtight container. This is best when it is made a day ahead of time.

🌾 *Gluten-Free Variation:* This recipe is naturally gluten-free.

Index